The
Heart
Book

The HEART BOOK

A program for prevention of heart attack
from researchers at the
DUKE UNIVERSITY MEDICAL CENTER

Coordinator: Siegfried Heyden, M.D.

Belair
PUBLISHING COMPANY INC.

Copyright © 1981 by
Delair Publishing Company, Inc.
420 Lexington Avenue
New York, New York 10170

All rights reserved under the International and Pan-American
Copyright Conventions. Manufactured in the United States of
America and published simultaneously in Canada.

ISBN: 0-8326-2249-4

The Authors

James A. Blumenthal, Ph.D.
Assistant Clinical Professor of Medical Psychology, Division of Medical Psychiatry, Department of Psychiatry, Duke University Medical Center

William DeMaria, M.D.
Clinical Professor, Department of Pediatrics, Duke University Medical Center

Siegfried Heyden, M.D.
Professor, Department of Community and Family Medicine, Duke University Medical Center

Carole S. Orleans, Ph.D.
Assistant Professor, Division of Psychosomatic Medicine, Department of Psychiatry, Duke University Medical Center

Robert H. Shipley, Ph.D.
Associate Professor, Division of Medical Psychology, Department of Psychiatry, Duke University Medical Center

R. Sanders Williams, M.D.
Assistant Professor, Division of Cardiology, Department of Medicine, Duke University Medical Center

Contents

Introduction

Heart Attack and Lifestyle: A Question of Mindless Habit Versus Informed Choice

R. Sanders Williams, M.D.

Despite the many upsetting features of contemporary life such as crime, inflation, environmental pollution and social injustice which weigh upon us all, many modern Americans really do enjoy an almost unprecedented freedom of personal choice in governing the conduct of our day-to-day lives. Although most of us have some limitations over the choice of where we live, or how we earn our livelihood, we exercise nearly complete personal freedom over the aspects of our daily existences which have come to be known as "lifestyle": what we eat, what widespread habits (cigarette, alcohol, or other drug use) we accept or reject, and how we spend the increasing proportion of our time which is devoted to leisure activities. It is entirely proper that the elements of a person's "lifestyle", to the degree to which no other person's rights are compromised, should be entirely under that individual's control. Even if a person chooses life habits which may bring him (or her) physical harm, traditional Western concepts of individual freedom give him the right to do so, as long as he brings no harm to other individuals. Our efforts to persuade the readers of this book to alter certain life habits which we believe may be harmful stem from our observations that many persons are *not* making free and informed choices regarding their lifestyle: they are either victims of habit, or have made life choices on the basis of erroneous information.

Although we do not understand the ultimate "causes" of coronary heart disease and heart attack at this time, and we do not understand the details of the relationship between dietary fat or lack of exercise and heart disease, the evidence linking lifestyle habits in industrialized nations to coronary heart disease is simply too overwhelming to ignore.

We realize that your uncle may have smoked 2 packs of cigarettes per day, consumed all the salt, cholesterol and saturated fat he liked, and walked from the dining room table to the television as his only exercise, yet lived to be 94, while your friend with no risk factors died iast year with a heart attack at age 43. We can't explain such undoubtedly real examples on the basis of current knowledge. However, we can say definitely that such cases are exceptions to the general patterns, which studies of thousands of persons around the world have revealed in the past 3 decades. There is little question that if you choose the life habits that have been associated with heart attacks (the "risk factors" you'll read so much about in the following chapters) you must accept an increased risk of developing coronary heart disease.

It's possible that a well-informed rational person may choose to take risks. A well-known Supreme Court justice of recent times was an avid mountain climber; he rationally accepted the risks involved because of the enjoyment it brought him. In the same manner, a person may continue to smoke cigarettes, to lead a sedentary lifestyle, or to eat foods which we regard as potentially harmful. Our only plea is that such decisions be made consciously, not by mindless habit, with full access by the individual to whatever information may be available to make the decision.

The authors of this book have attempted, in as unbiased a manner as possible, to provide the readers with a distillation of the scientific information that exists today regarding the relationships. between life habits and heart attack. High blood pressure, high blood sugar, high blood cholesterol, cigarette smoking, obesity, physical inactivity, and excessive emotional stress all increase one's risk for heart attack, yet in most cases can be normalized simply by a different choice of lifestyle. A reduction in risk factors is no guarantee against the development of heart attack: there are certain features like family history which influence heart attack risk which are beyond an individual's control. This fact of life is, however, a weak argument for failing to eliminate the risk factors which *are* reversible.

Americans have done impressive things over the past 15 years. They have definitely changed their eating patterns, from a high animal fat diet to more sensible nutrition. They are smoking less and exercising more: one American in three now participates in some form of regular exercise. They have learned to control blood pressure - at least 70% of all hypertensives are now under good control. (And with these profound changes in lifestyle, the United States is the first country in the world where the epidemic of heart attack deaths has been reported to decline markedly.)

It is our desire that this encouraging trend towards lower rates of death and disability from coronary heart disease be extended. We stated earlier that a major goal of this book is to supply readers with important information on which to base informed and conscious choices over their lifestyle. A second major goal, assuming that many of our readers will indeed choose to reduce risk factors for coronary heart disease, is to give them the tools for making these changes: practical techniques for smoking cessation, beginning an exercise program, controlling stress in their lives, controlling high blood pressure, and eating prudently. The ultimate goal is an active participation by individuals in their own health, and a further decline in tragic and premature death and disability due to coronary heart disease.

Fig. 1. Percent Change in Mortality Rates
United States, 1968 to 1976
Persons Age 35-74, by Sex-Race

Cause of Death	Percent Change, 1968 to 1976, by sex-color				
	white men	white women	non-white men	non-white women	all
Coronary heart disease	-21.0%	-26.5%	-30.7%	-39.1%	-24.3%
Cerebro-vascular disease	30.6%	30.4%	43.7%	47.1%	32.7%
Major CV diseases	-20.9%	-26.1%	-33.2%	-40.7%	-24.6%
All causes	-15.3%	-16.4%	-24.8%	-32.7%	-17.3%

1

Smoking and the Heart

Siegfried Heyden, M.D.

Cigarette smoking and inhaling cause nicotine to flow through the coronary arteries (the major blood vessels supplying the heart muscle with oxygen). Smoking a cigarette usually takes approximately 10 minutes. This is sufficient time for our coronary arteries to be flooded with nicotine. The next step follows almost instantaneously: the nicotine mobilizes a hormone from our adrenal glands. The adrenal glands are very small, situated above the kidneys on the left and right side. The adrenal glands produce a hormone called adrenalin.

As soon as adrenalin is mobilized, it enters the blood stream and flows along in the coronary arteries, causing two major effects on the heart muscle: (1) the heart works much faster and harder. We can measure the additional work load on the heart muscle by an increase in the pulse rate and some increase in blood pressure. This happens because adrenalin acts like a "whip" on the heart muscle. (2) the heart, like any muscle that works hard and fast, *uses more oxygen*. This is where the real problem starts.

Under normal circumstances (non-smoking), each red blood cell carries hemoglobin, the red color of the red blood cells combined with oxygen. This oxygen is much needed in every cell of the heart muscle, particularly when the muscle is working hard. When the heart is getting a "whipping" from the hormone adrenalin, it re-

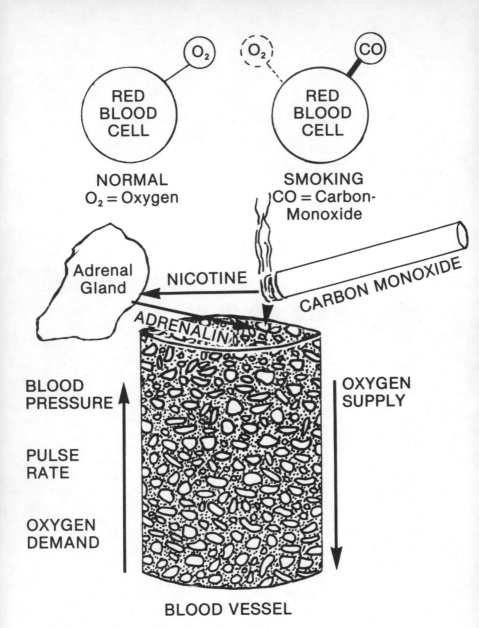

Fig. 2.
Presently, there is no evidence that chronic cigarette smoke inhalation may cause degenerative changes in the coronary arteries. Also this hypothesis would not fit with the clinical and epidemiological observation that ex-smokers experience a lowering of their risk for the development of CHD within a relatively short time. The reason why cigarette smoking causes excess rates of myocardial infarction and sudden death may be in part explained by Fig. 2.

quires even more oxygen. However, unfortunately, during the act of smoking, we are also inhaling a lot of carbon monoxide. This carbon monoxide has a tremendous power to affiliate with the hemoglobin in the red blood cell. The oxygen molecule is pushed out. This new complex of hemoglobin and carbon monoxide deprives the heart muscle of the oxygen, which it needs so badly under the "whipping" action of adrenalin.

The reason why so many heavy smokers die a sudden death, or suffer from myocardial infarction much more than non-smokers, is the tremendous discrepancy between the increased oxygen *demand* under hard work and the decreased oxygen *supply* because of the carbon monoxide replacing oxygen in the red blood cells.

Smoking has only a temporary, but deadly, effect on the heart muscle and the coronary arteries. A smoker can decrease his risk of heart attack or sudden death in a very short time if he quits smoking. This is the reason for the following chapter.

2

Take Heart, There Are Ways to Quit Smoking

Carole S. Orleans, Ph.D.
Robert H. Shipley, Ph.D.

People usually try to scare you into quitting smoking. They point to the dire long-range effects of smoking on health. And, in fact, smoking *is* a serious health threat. But you already know that smoking is bad for your health. When people continually tell you that you're killing yourself, it can increase your feelings of helplessness and anger. Many smokers respond to such pressure by saying "I'd rather live less time and be happy while I'm here." We agree that the quality of your life is important, but we also know that your life will rapidly improve if you decide to invest the work and time necessary to learn to be an ex-smoker. We want you to be happy *and* live longer. Wouldn't you be happy to breathe easier, have more energy on less sleep, have a younger complexion, rid yourself of cigarette odors, be able to taste and smell better, sleep better, and digest your food better with less stomach upset? Wouldn't you like to have a lower heart rate, and be able to work harder with less sweat? And what about coughing? Perhaps more important, when you quit smoking you will feel justifiably proud of freeing yourself of an enslaving addiction, and for presenting a good example to your children. As part of the bargain, you will also drastically reduce your risk of suffering dread diseases such as heart attcks, lung cancer, bronchitis and emphysema. Best of all, you will feel better as a nonsmoker.

But what about the suffering it takes to quit, the uncomfortable urges for a cigarette, the irritability, anxiety and difficulty in concentrating? When they quit smoking, many people do suffer some of these withdrawal symptoms. They occur primarily because of a dependency on the nicotine in cigarettes. But negative withdrawal symptoms are by no means universal. Many chronic smokers are surprised to find how easy this withdrawal phase can be. Furthermore, what most people don't realize is that these unpleasant reactions are strong for only a week or two. It takes three to seven days for your body to rid itself of most nicotine. This may account for the rapid reduction of urges and psychological "pain" over the first week. When people first quit smoking they often say, "If I have to suffer this much, I'd rather smoke and take the consequences." But the fact is that most of the suffering is over after only one week! And though you will certainly continue to have urges to smoke after stopping for a week, you will also begin to notice improvements in your health by then.

Why do some urges continue even after the nicotine is out of your system? We believe it's because the habit is strong and because you have so frequently smoked in pleasurable situations. After thousands of pairings with pleasurable situations, cigarettes acquire some of the pleasure of these situations. For example, you smoke while taking a break from work, while having coffee or a drink, during pleasant social conversation, after sex, and while relaxing. The cigarette takes on some of the pleasure of these things. In fact, much of the pleasure that you may now believe comes from the cigarette, actually comes from the associated activity—from taking a break, or taking a relaxing deep breath. The urges you will experience in situations where you normally would smoke take some time to diminish. For example, finishing a good meal may produce an urge for a cigarette for three months or longer. These urges do become less and less frequent, until they are rare.

Many people believe that quitting is all a matter of willpower. They may say, "I don't have much willpower when it comes to cigarettes." However, we know that quitting smoking is a matter of *using skills* to combat smoking urges and to replace the smoking habit. These are skills that you have, or can learn. In learning to ride a bike, it's common to feel unsteady and to fall frequently. This is, of course, because the novice rider doesn't have many bike-riding skills. Such skills come with coaching and practice. The same is true of nonsmoking. With our coaching and your practice you can learn to be an expert nonsmoker. There is no willpower here, only intelligent learning of skills through practice.

Once you do decide to stop smoking, you must decide when. The timing would be poor if you are in the midst of unusual crisis and turmoil, or if you are feeling extremely depressed or lonely. Of course, we all know smokers who never find the "right time". We're not saying to wait for that too rare moment when your life is completely calm and tranquil. But if you are honestly feeling quite blue and depressed, now is not the time to quit. There is one exception to this. If your doctor tells you that you must quit immediately for health reasons, then you must quit now, regardless of the level of stress in your life. If you are under a lot of stress or are depressed, but must quit now, we suggest you seek guidance from a medical or mental health professional (psychologist, physician, psychiatrist, or social worker) who is knowledgeable about quitting smoking. In chapter 10, we discuss how to find professional help.

You should know that the authors of this chapter are both former smokers who required several attempts to successfully break the habit. We know that it's difficult to really decide to quit smoking. We know that while part of you wants to break the habit, another part of you loves to smoke and doesn't want to give up that pleasure. Perhaps you can't imagine living without cigarettes, or hate to "desert" your smoking buddies. However, we believe you can become an ex-smoker if you follow the suggestions in this chapter.

From now on, we will assume that you have decided to quit.

We will discuss quitting in three equally important stages:

    preparing to quit

    quitting and

    remaining a non-smoker.

We will outline a three-stage program for quitting on your own with the help of this chapter. Most people who have quit smoking have quit on their own "cold turkey," used a variety of specific quitting techniques and benefited from the encouragement and support of family and friends. The program outlined in this chapter includes techniques used by such people, and in professionally-led quit-smoking programs. In fact, people who succeed in quitting on their own use methods that turn out to be pretty similar to those used in professionally-run programs.

Whether you quit on your own, or with the benefit of a formal quitting program, the basic principles and techniques are similar. So let personal preference and past experience be your guide. Under some circumstances, it may be desirable to start your quitting campaign in an organized stop-smoking program:

● You have already tried repeatedly to quit on your own *using a systematic approach.* You think that you'll really do better with the outside structure and support a program can offer—particularly when you have little support from friends and family for quitting:

● You think you will need professional help.

In any case, this chapter can be used as a resource. Also,

Fig. 3. CHECK OUT YOUR CIGARETTES

TAR AND NICOTINE CONTENT
OF CIGARETTES
Federal Trade Commission, May 1978
Ranked from low (1) to high (167)

NF —Non Filter (all others have filters)
M —Menthol
HP —Hard Pack
L —Lemon

RANK (tar)	BRAND	TYPE	TAR (mg)	NICO-TINE (mg)
62	Alpine	King, M	14	0.8
25	American Lights	120mm	8	0.7
28	American Lights	120mm, M	9	0.7
64	Belair	King, M	15	0.9
87	Belair	100mm, M	16	1.1
4	Benson & Hedges	Reg. (HP)	1	0.1
101	Benson & Hedges	King (HP)	17	1.2
112	Benson & Hedges 100's	100mm (HP)	17	1.1
103	Benson & Hedges 100's	100mm, M(HP)	17	1.1
115	Benson & Hedges 100's	100mm	17	1.1
111	Benson & Hedges 100's	100mm, M	17	1.0
165	Bull Durham	King	30	2.0
158	Camel	Reg., NF	25	1.6
131	Camel	King	19	1.3
1	Carlton	King (HP)	0.5	0.05
6	Carlton	King	1	0.1
2	Carlton	King, M	1	0.1
9	Carlton	100mm	4	0.4
145	Chesterfield	Reg. NF	23	1.3
163	Chesterfield	King, NF	28	1.7
108	Chesterfield	King	17	1.1
109	Chesterfield	101mm	17	1.1
12	Decade	King	5	0.4
13	Decade	King, M	5	0.4
48	Doral	King	12	0.9
45	Doral	King, M	12	0.8
73	DuMaurier	King (HP)	16	1.1
147	English Ovals	Reg., NF (HP)	23	1.6
166	English Ovals	King, NF (HP)	30	2.1
78	Eve	100mm	16	1.0
71	Eve	100mm, M	16	1.0
60	Eve 120's	120mm (HP)	14	1.0
66	Eve 120's	120mm, M (HP)	15	1.1
49	Fact	King	12	0.8
51	Fact	King, M	13	0.9
162	Fatima	King, NF	28	1.7
72	Galaxy	King	16	1.0
154	Half & Half	King	24	1.5
164	Herbert Tareyton	King, NF	29	1.8
35	Hi-Life	100mm (HP)	10	0.7
143	Home Run	Reg., HF	21	1.5
7	Iceberg 100's	100mm, M	3	0.3
67	Kent	King (HP)	15	1.0
85	Kent	King	16	1.1
50	Kent Micronite II	King	12	0.9
21	Kent Golden Lights	King	8	0.7
27	Kent Golden Lights	King, M	9	0.7
127	Kent	100mm	18	1.3
59	Kent Micronite II	100mm	14	1.0
33	Kent Golden Lights	100mm	9	0.8
98	Kent	100mm, M	17	1.1
30	Kent Golden Lights	100mm, M	9	0.8
14	King Sano	King	6	0.3
15	King Sano	King, M	6	0.3
142	Kool	Reg., NF, M	20	1.3
119	Kool	King, M (HP)	18	1.4
104	Kool	King, M	17	1.4
61	Kool Milds	King, M	14	0.9
123	Kool	100mm, M	18	1.3
91	L&M	King (HP)	17	1.0
93	L&M	King	17	1.0
19	L&M Lights	King	7	0.6
94	L&M	100mm	17	1.1
20	L&M Lights	100mm	8	0.6
124	L&M	100mm, M	18	1.1
141	L.T.Brown	120mm	20	1.5
133	L.T.Brown	120mm, M	19	1.4
107	Lark	King	17	1.1
132	Lark	100mm	19	1.2
96	Long Johns	120mm	17	1.3
80	Long Johns	120mm, M	16	1.3
150	Lucky Strike	Reg., NF	24	1.4
26	Lucky Ten	King	9	0.7
8	Lucky 100's	100mm	3	0.3
160	Mapleton	Reg., NF	27	1.2
151	Mapleton	King	24	1.4
100	Marlboro	King (HP)	17	1.0
58	Marlboro	King, M (HP)	14	0.8
113	Marlboro	King	17	1.0
40	Marlboro Lights	King	12	0.8
83	Marlboro	King, M	14	0.8

RANK (tar)	BRAND	TYPE	TAR (mg)	NICO-TINE (mg)
102	Marlboro	100mm (HP)	17	1.1
120	Marlboro	100mm	18	1.1
99	Max	120mm	17	1.3
114	Max	120mm, M	17	1.3
24	Merit	King	8	0.6
23	Merit	King, M	8	0.6
40	Merit 100's	100mm	11	0.7
39	Merit 100's	100mm, M	11	0.7
116	Montclair	King, M	17	1.3
148	More	120mm	23	1.7
149	More	120mm, M	23	1.7
52	Multifilter	King	13	0.8
41	Multifilter	King, M	11	0.7
106	Newport	King, M (HP)	17	1.2
122	Newport	King, M	18	1.3
34	Newport Lights	King, M	10	0.8
135	Newport	100mm	19	1.4
3	Now	King, (HP)	2	0.1
5	Now	King, M (HP)	2	0.1
126	Oasis	King, M	18	1.1
139	Old Gold Straights	Reg., NF	20	1.2
156	Old Gold Straights	King, NF	25	1.5
86	Old Gold Filters	King (HP)	16	1.1
125	Old Gold Filters	King	18	1.2
144	Old Gold 100's	100mm	21	1.4
159	Pall Mall	King, NF	26	1.6
110	Pall Mall	King	17	1.2
16	Pall Mall Extra Mild	King	7	0.5
128	Pall Mall	100mm	19	1.4
69	Pall Mall	100mm, M	16	1.2
29	Parliament	King (HP)	9	0.6
32	Parliament	King	9	0.6
47	Parliament 100's	100mm	12	0.8
140	Phillip Morris	Reg., NF	20	1.1
157	Phillip Morris Commander	King, NF	25	1.4
97	Phillip Morris International	100mm (HP)	17	1.1
62	Phillip Morris International	100mm, M (HP)	16	1.0
146	Picayune	Reg., NF	23	1.6
152	Piedmont	Reg., NF	24	1.4
167	Players	Reg., NF (HP)	35	2.5
153	Raleigh	King, NF	24	1.4
75	Raleigh	King	16	1.0
54	Raleigh Lights	King	13	0.9
105	Raleigh	100mm	17	1.2
31	Real	King	9	0.7
22	Real	King, M	8	0.6
89	St. Moritz	100mm	16	1.1
95	St. Moritz	100mm, M	17	1.1
118	Salem	King, M (HP)	18	1.2
84	Salem	King, M	16	1.1
38	Salem Lights	King, M	10	0.8
129	Salem	100mm, M	19	1.3
36	Salem Long Lights	100mm, M	10	0.8
70	Sano	Reg., NF	16	0.5
65	Saratoga	120mm (HP)	15	1.0
68	Saratoga	120mm, M (HP)	16	1.0
81	Silva Thins	100mm	16	1.2
74	Silva Thins	100mm, M	16	1.1
137	Spring 100's	100mm, M	20	1.1
161	Stratford	King, NF	28	1.1
155	Stratford	King	25	1.4
117	Tall	120mm	17	1.4
78	Tall	120mm, M	16	1.3
92	Tareyton	King	17	1.2
18	Tareyton Lights	King	7	0.6
88	Tareyton	100mm	16	1.2
17	Tempo	King	7	0.5
10	True	King	5	0.4
11	True	King, M	5	0.4
55	True 100's	100mm	13	0.8
56	True 100's	100mm, M	13	0.8
90	Twist	100mm, L/M	17	1.3
43	Vantage	King	11	0.8
42	Vantage	King, M	11	0.8
37	Vantage	100mm	10	0.8
83	Viceroy	King	16	1.1
44	Viceroy Extra Mild	King	11	0.8
121	Viceroy	100mm	18	1.2
77	Virginia Slims	100mm	16	0.9
76	Virginia Slims	100mm, M	16	0.9
134	Winston	King (HP)	19	1.3
138	Winston	King	20	1.3
53	Winston Lights	King	13	0.9
136	Winston	100mm	19	1.3
57	Winstone Lights 100's	100mm	13	1.0
130	Winston	100mm, M	19	1.3

U.S. Department of Health, Education and Welfare/Public Health Service Office on Smoking and Health

Chapter 10 gives information on nonsmoking clinics which may be available in your area. The self-help techniques we recommend will be valuable to you, and can help you choose a sound quitting program.

Preparing to Quit

Careful preparation is one key to success. This is as important in becoming a nonsmoker as it is in giving a good speech, or winning a prize fight. Getting ready to quit starts with peaking your motivation and the expectation that you will succeed.

You might want to see your family doctor for a checkup that focuses on conditions or functions that are likely to improve rapidly after quitting (e.g. shortness of breath, wheezing, loss of stamina.) Tell your doctor you're planning to quit, and discuss ways that he or she can help to monitor your progress. Sometimes smokers who have not been explicitly told to quit by their physicians assume that their doctor thinks it is okay for them to continue smoking. Unfortunately, not all physicians discuss the personal risks of smoking, or give firm advice to quit. Until recently, the cigarette habit and ways to break it have not been well understood. Doctors sometimes hesitate in giving strong quitting advice, fearing their patients could not quit (untrue), or fearing they would not be able to follow through personally and offer needed help (often true). Talk it over with your doctor. He or she can be an invaluable ally even without offering specific advice about how to quit. Encouragement and enthusiasm about your efforts to improve your health, and crucial information about your body's response to smoking and quitting are alone invaluable.

Expect to succeed even before you quit. This is very important. Friends who are ex-smokers can give you vital support and encouragement. They can tell you what to expect and are living proof that you can succeed and enjoy being a non-smoker. If you count few ex-smokers among your friends, maybe your local chapter of the American Cancer Society has organized a telephone "Quit-line"—a hotline staffed by ex-smokers—for additional information and inspiration. If you truly doubt your ability to succeed, we recommend a very readable paperback *You Can Stop* (Pocket Books, New York, 1977) written by Jacquelyn Rogers, an ex-smoker and the co-founder of SmokEnders, one of the largest commercial quit-smoking programs. This book can help you re-evaluate your ability to quit. One suggestion it makes is to list the benefits you expect from quitting. Rogers lists 150 non-health-related benefits. Anticipating benefits and posting a list in a prominent place, such as on your bathroom mirror, makes good sense. People who succeed at quitting seem more motivated to achieve quitting benefits than to avoid smoking harms.

Analyze your smoking habit. For at least two typical days (one weekday and one weekend day) *keep a list of the circumstances in which you light up a cigarette* (use an index card that fits into your cigarette pack.) What are you doing? What activity are you turning away from, or completing? How are you feeling when you light up? And after you finish the cigarette? (Many smokers who think they smoke to "feel better" are surprised to find they don't really feel much different after a cigarette.) Look over these lists. When do you smoke? If you are like most smokers, there are some situations in which you almost always smoke: after meals, for example, when hard at work, when you are tense, in a new social gathering. There are other situations in which you rarely smoke—during outdoor activities or when you're with your children. Knowing your high-risk situations helps you prepare for the quitting stage. For example, you'll need to plan *new rituals for ending meals or taking a work break.* You'll need to know when to be especially on guard to prevent or reduce cravings. Knowing your smoking circumstances also helps you figure out what you get out of smoking—does it relax you, give you something to do with your hands, punctuate your activities? The National Cancer Institute (Office of Cancer Communications, Bethesda, Maryland, 20205) will send you, free of charge, a *Helping Smokers Quit Kit* that includes a *Why Do You Smoke* questionnaire with eighteen questions to get at six motivations for smoking: stimulation, handling, pleasurable relaxation, tension reduction, psychological cravings and habit. Clarifying your reasons for smoking can also help you choose meaningful replacements. If you smoke chiefly to relax, for example, you'll need another relaxing habit. If, instead, your smoking is mainly a nervous habit or a means of keeping your hands busy, then doodling, worry beads, or bending a paper clip might be replacements.

To quit cold turkey—set a target quit date three to four weeks from now. Avoid having your quit date fall at a stressful time, such as the date you are to move, change jobs, or pay your tax bill. Quit abruptly on this date. Increase your chances of success, by planning less stressful activities for your first quit week and by including more non-tempting activities, and plenty of tender loving care from family and friends.

Reduce nicotine dependency. Nicotine dependency or addiction plays a major role in most people's smoking habit. Cigarette cravings are associated with drops in your body's nicotine level. Withdrawal symptoms during quitting are caused by nicotine loss.

There are ways to minimize your nicotine dependency before quitting. But, ultimately we recommend "cold turkey" quitting because withdrawal symptoms such as irritability and anxiety are actually *less* severe than with gradual cutting down of the number of cigarettes. This is because cravings are related to residual nicotine, and beyond a certain level, nicotine is removed faster and more completely with abrupt quitting. Another problem with gradual cutting down is that most people can't get below 10-12 much-craved, much-enjoyed cigarettes each day.

To minimize your nicotine dependency before quitting, we suggest either of two optimal strategies. First, you can gradually cut down to 10-12 cigarettes daily, and practice coping with resisted smoking urges. But then, quit abruptly without trying to further gradually reduce your smoking. Another strategy is to smoke your usual number of cigarettes, but switch brands to reduce cutting your nicotine level by 30% each week until, after 4 weeks, you reach 10% of your usual level. At this point, you should quit abruptly. To use this "nicotine fading" program consult the

---

Fig. 4
Nicotine Fading Program[1]

Baseline week: Normal brand_____
                    Nicotine Baseline per cigarette_____mg

Week 2: 30% reduction from Normal Brand
    Baseline level *(above)* =
$$\underline{\qquad \text{x .70} \qquad}$$
    New nicotine level =   mg per cigarette
    Suggested Brands:_____

Week 3: 60% reduction from Normal Brand
    Baseline level *(above)* =
$$\underline{\qquad \text{x .40} \qquad}$$
    New nicotine level =   mg per cigarette
    Suggested Brands:_____

Week 4: 90% reduction from Normal Brand
    Baseline level *(above)* =
$$\underline{\qquad \text{x .10} \qquad}$$
    New nicotine level =   mg per cigarette
    Suggested Brands:_____

Weeks: Quit "Cold Turkey"

Federal Trade Commission Table on pages 20-21 and find the nicotine level of your present brand. Then use this value in the equations on the chart in Fig. 4. that outline this program. You will have a choice of several brands, menthol and non-menthol, at each level. This program applies only if you are not already smoking the lowest nicotine and tar brands. You must keep track of how many cigarettes you smoke at each level to make sure you are smoking the same number, and not increasing your cigarette consumption. We suggest the form in Fig. 4. for this purpose. This program works best if you can review your weekly progress with someone who knows the goals of the program and will be enthusiastic about your success: your spouse, your doctor, an ex-smoking friend, a work associate. Finally, be sure to stick to your "quit date". Beware not to settle on reduced smoking or reduced nicotine intake. Remember, there is no "safe smoking." Both these cut down procedures are preparation for total quitting.

The last element of being prepared to quit involves practicing a

Self-Monitoring

Be sure to keep a daily talley of the cigarettes you smoke each week. Avoid increasing the number of cigarettes you smoke. Review this talley with someone close to you or your doctor.

Daily nicotine counts
Week beginning_____
Brand _____
Nictoine per Cigarette_____mg.

	Monday: _____		_____
	Tuesday:_____		_____
Total #	Wednesday: _____	Total	_____
cigarettes	Thursday: _____	nicotine	_____
	Friday:_____	intake	_____
	Saturday: _____		_____
	Sunday: _____		_____

[1]Based on R. M. Foxx and R. A. Brown, Nicotine fading and self-monitoring for cigarette abstinence or controlled smoking. *Journal of Applied Behavior Analysis* 1979, *12*, 111-125.

relaxation technique. Later, you can use this technique to reduce the tension often associated with withdrawal and to control and resist smoking urges. Chapter 6 presents several relaxation techniques. We recommend "taking a breather." Slow, regular, deep abdominal breathing, in contrast to quick, shallow, chest breathing, helps you to feel and be physically relaxed. Relaxed breathing must be learned. Try it. Assume a comfortable position in your chair. Place one hand on your abdomen, the other on your chest. Take in a deep breath through your nose. Hold it a few seconds, then exhale slowly through your mouth with a slight blowing motion, saying to yourself "relax." Feel the hand on your abdomen rise and fall with each breath while the hand on your chest is relatively motionless. Repeat this several times. Notice how refreshed you feel. The oxygen you breathe in causes a high, almost like that first puff of a cigarette. Taking a breather, like lighting a cigarette, involves a momentary rest break which in itself can be relaxing. Practice taking 2-3 abdominal breaths 20-30 times a day until it feels natural. Use events in your day to remind you to "take a breather." For example, each time the phone rings, take a breather; when you are at a stop light, take a breather. What things happen frequently in your day which you can use as a reminder to do this relaxed breathing? With practice, it will become automatic. Many people like to imagine a relaxing scene (the beach, a mountain stream) when they "take a breather." Used regularly, this relaxation will not only help you stay off cigarettes, but can help with tension problems such as headaches, irritability or fatigue.

Quitting

The quitting phase generally lasts as long as nicotine withdrawal—about two weeks. In this phase, you'll be combatting the most frequent and intensive urges to smoke. Therefore you'll need maximum quitting skills and outside support. The first week will be the hardest. During this week, remind yourself that the unpleasant feeling and urges will pass, and that each day off cigarettes is an investment in an easier second week, and a satisfying smoke-free future. In this section, we'll prepare you for the worst—anticipating a difficult (but short and tolerable) withdrawal phase. But, you should know that as many as 40%-50% of ex-smokers in several surveys reported no withdrawal effects! *Quitting smoking may be far easier than you ever expected.*

Quitting is not a matter of having willpower. It is a matter of using systematic methods to head off smoking urges or to ride them out when they occur, and to find satisfying positive cigarette substitutes. Positive thinking, pampering yourself and getting enough praise and encouragement from family and friends are also important.

There are several definite strategies for heading off or reducing urges to light up. First, *temporarily avoid high-risk smoking circumstances* (like card playing) *when you can* and at the same time, spend more time in situations where you don't smoke (the shower, movies, outdoors). Do things that would make you less interested in smoking (e.g. brushing your teeth). Eat balanced protein-rich meals avoiding sugary or starchy (carbohydrate) snacks which elevate blood sugar but then cause it to drop creating the "sugar blues" and an associated cigarette craving. Practice "taking a breather" often—especially when you have an urge to light up. Get at least fifteen minutes of exercise each day (e.g. walking, bike riding, swimming). Increase relaxing activities and cut down on coffee and other stimulants. This will help you reduce the tension associated with nicotine withdrawal. Focus on your success rather than on any slips you may experience or on the difficulties of quitting (e.g. "I'm so pleased for going sixteen hours without a cigarette" versus "I'd walk a mile for a Camel, Vantage, Virginia Slim, etc.).

Smoke-proof your home and work area to help prevent smoking slips. Get rid of ashtrays and cigarettes that would tempt you. Some people resist doing this, feeling that they should be strong enough to resist temptation. Don't fall into this trap. If you were on a diet, you wouldn't keep chocolate cake around. It's best to resist temptation, and don't forget to smoke-proof your car, your gym locker, your bureau drawers, etc. It is important not to allow yourself even one cigarette, since this frequently leads to a pack and back to being a smoker. However, if you do slip and smoke a cigarette, figure out how the slip came about and write down a plan for dealing with this tempting situation the next time. Close your eyes and actually imagine yourself using a coping technique to avoid smoking in the future, and remember you're still a nonsmoker.

Experiment with a variety of smoking substitutes: "taking a breather", doodling, worry beads, crossword puzzles, chewing sugarless gum, munching on carrot and celery sticks or sunflower seeds, sucking on a low-calorie candy like Velamints or chewing on a Stim-U-Dent or toothpick. Choose substitutes that make sense for you. Don't expect the replacement to be as enjoyable as the cigarette in the beginning. But, over time, the activities you choose can become as relaxing and enjoyable as smoking. After all, smoking in the beginning was not all that enjoyable either.

One substitute—food—deserves special attention. Many new ex-smokers gain 5-10 lbs. Metabolism changes may cause part of this gain. But changes in eating habits are the chief causes. During the quitting phase (and after), have plenty of healthy low-calorie snacks around, attractively prepared and ready to eat (carrot sticks, radish "roses", fresh fruit). Choose low calorie candies and sugarless gums. Eat regular protein-rich meals to avoid the "sugar blues" and excessive hunger. It doesn't take much preventive work to avoid troublesome gains. For additional guidance, order the American Cancer Society's free booklet "Slim and Smokeless" (7370 Greenville Avenue, Dallas, Texas 75231) and see Chapter 7 in this volume. If you should gain weight, don't give up on quitting. Sometimes people will think smoking is less important than being over-weight. If controlling your weight is generally a problem, it will take some work whether you quit smoking or not. And if it is not a problem for you, it should be easy to shed those few extra pounds once you're comfortable with your new status as a nonsmoker.

We can't stress too much how important it is to get outside support and encouragement. People who've succeeded in quitting both on their own and in formal programs are much more likely than people who fail to experience support and understanding from family or friends. People close to you should understand what you are going through, how hard it is, and the importance of your commitment to a healthier lifestyle. Many people don't tell others when they are trying to quit, perhaps fearing to risk "public" failure or wanting to avoid unhelpful pressure. But smoking is a tough habit to break so we recommend asking close friends and family to offer daily support or encouragement in ways that you feel will be helpful. At a minimum, you should ask people close to you to agree (1) not to offer you cigarettes, (2) to frequently praise your effort and success and (3) to absolutely ignore any smoking slips.

You should also praise yourself. Self-congratulating thoughts are extremely important in quitting. Thoughts such as "I'm proud of myself for resisting smoking," can be listed on index cards to jog your memory when you are tempted to smoke. In fact, you should congratulate yourself not only for not smoking but also for using your new nonsmoking skills (such as "taking a breather"). You should use the money you save by not smoking to buy things to reward your nonsmoking: new clothes, flowers, movie or theater tickets, bicycle accessories, etc.

You will begin to see improvement in your physical condition as early as two days after you quit. You'll get winded less easily, have more energy and wheeze less. Sometimes coughing and phlegm production gets somewhat worse for two to three days before they improve as a result of the body ridding itself of tobacco smoke toxins. These and other "symptoms of recovery" are summarized in a two-page brochure included in the National Cancer Institute's Quit Kit mentioned earlier. If you have any special concerns or questions about these symptoms, call your doctor. Also, its a good idea to see your doctor several weeks after quitting to get the good news about your improved physical condition.

Remaining a Nonsmoker

Many people who succeed in quitting for a short time fall off the wagon when they stop using their nonsmoking self-control skills, when they start to rationalize to themselves why they should have a cigarette, or when they are not prepared to deal with "dangerous" tempting situations. A return to smoking is most likely in the first three months after quitting. But the new ex-smoker should remain "on guard" for at least six months to one year.

Relapse usually occurs not because people are continaully tempted to smoke, but as a way to deal with anger, frustration or a significant emotional stress. It's as if you say to yourself "I'll smoke to get rid of my anger (tension, etc.)". Conflict with other people is another high-risk relapse situation. Often people resort smoking in anger to "spite" someone close to them. Pressure from others to resume smoking also leads many exsmokers to take up the habit again. You will need tactful comebacks to people who try to get you to smoke ("No thanks, I'm a nonsmoker now" or "Please don't offer me cigarettes anymore, I'm working to stay a nonsmoker").

Temptation also comes from within, in the form of rationalizations for relapse. There are a number of these rationalizations: lack of confidence about your ability to stay off cigarettes (e.g. "I'm not the kind of person who can succeed"); an urge to test yourself (e.g. "If I'm *really* a nonsmoker, I can smoke one cigarette and put the habit down again"), nostalgia (e.g. "A cigarette right now would be *so* good, I'd feel so relaxed" or "so much better prepared to manage this crisis") and concern about some of the short-term unwanted changes that accompany quitting smoking ("If I smoke, I can control my weight").

To be fully prepared for all these temptations, you must have specific coping techniques and counter-arguments to use on yourself and on others. You can, for instance, "take a breather" when you need to relax, or write out actual rebuttals to your own tempting thoughts about how smoking will make you feel less angry, tense or help you over a conflict with someone or a stressful problem (e.g. "It's not true that if I smoke now I'll get rid of my anger. The cause of my anger will be the same, and I'll just be adding a sense of failure to my angry feelings").

Slipping and smoking a cigarette places an ex-smoker in a very vulnerable position. Most slips lead to full blown relapses, especially when the ex-smoker feels he or she is a total failure because of the slip. Drs. Marlatt and Gordon, psychologists who have carefully studied the relapse process stress that "one swallow does not make a summer." *(Behavioral Medicine: Changing Health Lifestyles.* N.Y.: Brunner-Mazel, 1979.)

A slip is not all that unusual. It does not mean that you failed or that you have lost control over your behavior. You will probably feel guilty about what you have done, and will blame yourself for having slipped. This feeling is to be expected; it is part of what we call the Abstinence Violation Effect. There is no reason why you have to give in to this feeling and continue to smoke. The feeling will pass in time. Look upon the slip as a single independent event, something which can be avoided in the future by the use of an appropriate coping response (pp. 447-448).

Attack directly any unwanted changes resulting from quitting smoking, so they do not become reasons for relapse, and so you can enjoy the deserved feelings of being in control and proud of your accomplishment.

If you have put on a troublesome amount of weight, start a weight control program. Chapter 7 outlines one program. You may want to join Weight Watchers, TOPS or another self-help weight loss program. If you continue to feel more anxious than usual, consult Chapter 6 which discusses the need to relax and effective relaxation techniques. A physical exercise program see in Chapter 4 can build on your new found stamina and sense of physical well-being.

If feelings of depression or deprivation related to the loss of cigarettes linger, take special care to pamper yourself. Marlatt and Gordon suggest classifying your daily activities as "shoulds" (things you do because you must) and "wants" (things you do for pleasure and enjoyment). For many smokers, cigarettes are "rewards", "wants" in a day filled with "shoulds". One way to prevent depression and relapse is to increase the other "wants" and decrease the "shoulds". A new hobby or increased exercise would provide an enriching outlet for your increased energy.

Like quitting smoking, staying off cigarettes and remaining a nonsmoker is not a matter of willpower or luck, but involves continuing to use the substitutes and methods you used to help you get off cigarettes. Likewise rewarding yourself for non-smoking and continuing your association with supportive ex-smoking allies can help seal your success over the long run.

If you should return to smoking, remember that this does not mean you are a "bad" or weak person. Smoking is a health issue, not a moral one. You may want to analyze how your return to smoking occurred. What went wrong? What would have helped? Then make a new plan of attack. You may wish to try the same approach, but at a period of less stress, or asking for more support from others. A more detailed step-by-step self-help quitting program may also be beneficial. We recommend either *Become an Ex-*

Smoker (Prentice Hall, 1978) by Drs. Danaher and Lichtenstein or the two-part manual (available from your local American Lung Association): *Freedom from Smoking in 20 Days* and *A Lifetime of Freedom from Smoking.* These manuals go beyond the present chapter in offering concrete suggestions for effective self-control strategies. Or you may wish to attend a quit clinic (see chapter 10) or see a professional quit smoking therapist. Group and therapist support, and even a slightly different approach can make an important difference. The most effective treatments, for example, combine training in the self-control techniques outlined in this chapter with unpleasant experiences with cigarettes to offset your positive feeling toward smoking. Most successful ex-smokers have tried at least once before to quit and have failed. Quitting seems to involve gradual, cumulative learning. So if you should return to smoking, take heart, there are still ways to stop smoking.

3

Cholesterol

Siegfried Heyden, M.D.
Barbara Stucky

The word "arteriosclerosis" which is identical with "atherosclerosis" or simply hardening of the arteries often leaves a patient with the mental image of his good old happily-ignored arteries having suddenly and mysteriously been transformed into a tangle of calcified pipes. The image is not far from reality, but the process is neither sudden nor mysterious. We will discuss how atherosclerosis leads to heart attacks.

There is a ranking order of risk factors for the development of heart attacks *(Fig. 5.)*.

Fig. 5. Ranking Order of Risk Factors for Coronary Heart Disease

1. Hypercholesterolemia
2. Cigarette smoke inhalation
3. Hypertension
4. Diabetes
5. Obesity
6. Hyperuricemia (or Gout)

A high blood-fat level (measured by cholesterol units in milligrams) is the major cause of the hardening—through thickening (sclerosis)—of the blood vessel walls. High blood-fat levels, called hypercholesterolemia—literally too much cholesterol in the blood, first manifest themselves as fatty yellow streaks in the thin walls of arteries, and gradually thicken the entire arterial wall. Thus the inner diameter or lumen of the arteries is narrowed, and at the same time hardened—therefore the name hardening of the

Fig. 6.

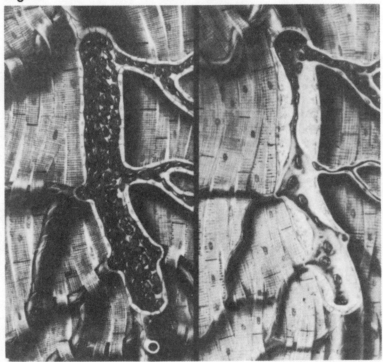

artery. (See *Fig. 6.* for a sectional view of a healthy, young, and a diseased artery.) With increasingly high levels of blood cholesterol, the vessel's lumen can become so restricted that hardly any red blood cells can carry nutrients and vital oxygen to the heart muscle and the body's organs. These greatly thickened areas of the vessel walls are called plaques and appear to the surgeon as a whitish-yellow mash-like material, which a microscope shows to be cholesterol crystals. After these cholesterol deposits have lodged in the blood vessel wall for a number of years, they will eventually be surrounded by calcium. The calcium deposits are the result of the body's vain attempt to neutralize the foreign bodies of the cholesterol crystals. By the time the disease has reached this stage, the plaques can no longer be reduced by diet or drugs.

Why Me?
It is at this stage that the patient begins to feel like Job: "Why me?" Well, generally speaking, our blood cholesterol level is predetermined by our genes. If our parents and grandparents had low or normal cholesterol levels, we stand a good chance of benefiting from this positive genetic inheritance. If, on the other hand, we are burdened with a family history of high cholesterol levels or even hypercholesterolemia, there is a very great risk of this metabolic disorder appearing in the second and third generations. This genetically determined abnormality is a strong indicator for severe blood vessel disease beginning at a young age. Survivors have transmitted the abnormality to the next generation before succumbing to a heart attack in their thirties or forties.

But the majority of mankind is *not* born with this inherited condition, and the widespread high cholesterol levels found in Western society are caused by the food we eat, the lives we lead, and a number of beloved bad habits. Most of our remote ancestors led physically hard lives on diets of root vegetables, full grain bread and legumes, the monotony of which was broken by the occasional feast of high-fat and protein rich foods. We, on the other hand, have the means to indulge ourselves on "rich men's meats" and, in consequence, are dying of the Western Society's excess risk factors.

From animal experiments it is well known that various species react differently to a high cholesterol diet, e.g., rats or dogs can consume inordinate amounts of animal fats and never develop arteriosclerosis of their arteries while rabbits or pigs may become hypercholesterolemic when fed some high cholesterol containing foods; and these animals are prone to develop severe degrees of arteriosclerosis just like those seen in man.

Cholesterol Tolerance
It should not be surprising to find human beings divided in those who show a great tolerance towards cholesterol and animal fats in the daily food intake and others, who not only react with high blood levels of cholesterol, but subsequently become the victims of the clinical manifestations of arteriosclerosis such as angina pectoris (chest pain on exertion), heart attack or extreme narrowing of the arteries of the legs, with the development of gangrene which eventually may lead to amputation.

Two Important Divisions of Cholesterol, HDL—LDL
Blood fats or lipids cannot float freely in the blood stream but are bound to proteins, and therefore, are called lipo-proteins.

Whereas total cholesterol concentration in the blood was used in the past and still remains a valuable predictor of heart disease, today we are able to divide the blood fat levels into two major components, the so-called LDL—and HDL—cholesterol. With a special instrument, it is possible to measure these lipoproteins in their degree of density. A substance called *"Low Density Lipo-proteins"* or *LDL* correlates to the total cholesterol level in the blood serum, that is: the higher the cholesterol level, the higher the LDL level (Fig. 7.). Everyone's blood contains both *"High Density Lipo-proteins"* or *HDL* as well as LDL. HDL contains almost 50% protein and less than ¼ cholesterol. HDL acts as a protection against arteriosclerotic heart disease. This means the higher the HDL-levels in the blood, the greater appears the protection from heart attacks.

This should not be surprising if one looks at all the factors listed in *Fig. 8.* which are presently known to increase HDL-levels.

LDL is just the reverse, with 50% cholesterol and less than ¼ protein *(Fig. 9.).* A close study of *Figs. 8. and 9.* shows interesting corollaries between HDL and LDL and the likelihood of coronary heart disease when HDL levels are low and LDL levels are high.

As the HDL table indicates, only race and sex obviously cannot be influenced. All the things we ought to do are listed on the left side. The ranking order of these factors is, admittedly, somewhat arbitrary and may vary from one individual to another. However,

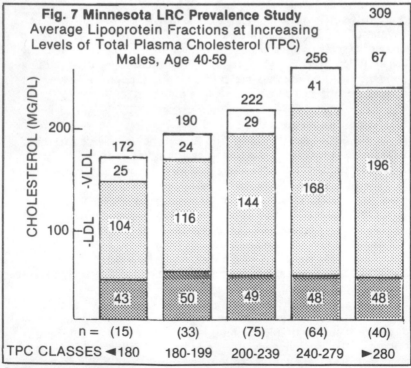

Dr. Blackburn et al: *Preventive Medicine* 8:612, 1979.

Fig. 8

HDL High/Increased	HDL Low/Reduced
black race	white race
females	males
normal weight	obesity
non- or ex-smoker	smoker
normal cholesterol levels	hypercholesterolemia
physical activity	physical inactivity
vegetables fats, oils	high animal fat diet
normal blood sugar levels	diabetes mellitus
low triglyceride levels	high triglyceride levels
children of healthy parents	children of CHD-patients
very moderate alcohol use	patients with heart attacks

Fig. 9

LDL High/Increased	LDL Low/Reduced
hypercholesterolemia	normal cholesterol level
white race	black race
males	females
impaired longevity	longevity
high animal fat diet	polyunsaturated fatty acids
smoker	non- or ex-smoker
physical inactivity	physical activity
patients with heart attacks	healthy persons

long-term studies carried out during the last ten years in American, Scandinavian and Israeli populations have unequivocally demonstrated the influence on HDL levels by normal weight, abstention from smoking, physical activity, preference of vegetable oils over animal fats and keeping blood sugar levels well under control. Intervention in any of the risk factors listed in the right half of *Fig. 8.* will not only increase HDL levels in the blood over a period of six months to one year, but will help to prevent coronary heart disease! When so many factors seem to play a role in the development of coronary heart disease, it would be foolish to expect any major impact on the prevention of coronary heart disease if one would attempt to influence only one single risk factor, for instance, to quit smoking but to continue consuming a diet high in animal fat and no exercise.

How can you tell whether a diet which contains large quantities of animal fats will leave you unscathed? Or will you develop high blood levels of cholesterol or even find yourself with the consequences of long-standing arteriosclerosis as angina pectoris, heart attacks or extreme narrowing of the leg arteries? Chances are that in your doctor's office the simple method of measuring total cholesterol levels is done and not the more complicated HDL - LDL determination.

Measurement and Value of Cholesterol in the Blood
There is only one reliable way to determine whether one's cholesterol level is low, normal or high: by taking two, or even three, blood samples within several days to get a good average of your baseline level. (The measurements in some laboratories are less reliable than in others; the difference between two blood cholesterol determinations should never exceed 20mg%.) Both newborn babies and animals have blood cholesterol levels of around 80 mg%. A normal cholesterol level in the blood serum for adults is defined as below 200 mg%, and an optimal adult level shows concentrations of between 180-200 mg%; those over 220 mg% need definite dietary treatment. Any cholesterol level above 260 mg% is dangerous and a vigorous program of weight normalization, elimination of animal fat and cholesterol from the food as well as a physical exercise program should be instituted. The above findings are based on a 10-year study of middle-aged men, originally free of heart disease, in seven different countries. Their baseline cholesterol levels at the onset of the study accurately predicted who developed fatal coronary disease and who did not *(Fig. 10.).* In human biology, with the exception of the corollary between smoking and lung cancer, there is no more accurate predictor for any other chronic disease than high baseline cholesterol levels and subsequent coronary deaths.

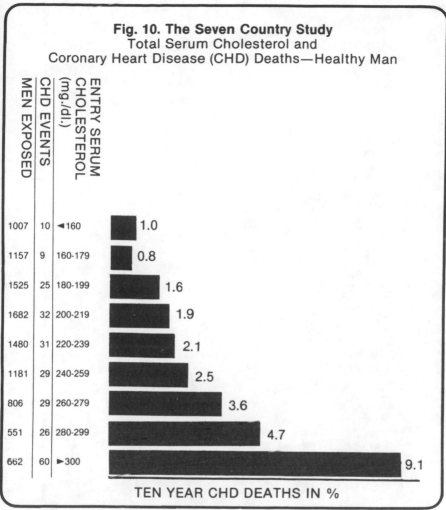

Fig. 10. The Seven Country Study
Total Serum Cholesterol and
Coronary Heart Disease (CHD) Deaths—Healthy Man

MEN EXPOSED	CHD EVENTS	ENTRY SERUM CHOLESTEROL (mg./dl.)	TEN YEAR CHD DEATHS IN %
1007	10	◄160	1.0
1157	9	160-179	0.8
1525	25	180-199	1.6
1682	32	200-219	1.9
1480	31	220-239	2.1
1181	29	240-259	2.5
806	29	260-279	3.6
551	26	280-299	4.7
662	60	►300	9.1

TEN YEAR CHD DEATHS IN %

Dr. Blackburn et al: *Preventive Medicine* 8:612, 1979.

One important aspect of the seven-country study was the correlation between customary diet and cholesterol levels. The diets of the men from Italy, Greece, and Yugoslavia were relatively high in vegetable fats and oils but much lower in animal fats than the diets of men from Holland, Finland, and the U.S.A. The cholesterol levels with the "Mediterranean Diet" were considerably lower than those of Northern European or American men, 40% of whose caloric intake is from animal origins. It has been proven that a lifelong overburdening of our metabolisms with diets high in animal fats is the major cause of diet-induced hypercholesterolemia and attendant coronary disease.

Fig. 11. Average cholesterol content in various food items (milligram/100 g = 3 ozs.)

Meat:

Pork (extra lean)	70
Beef (extra lean)	70
Veal (extra lean)	90
Mutton (extra lean)	65
Lamb (extra lean)	70
Venison	110

Inner Organs:

Pork liver	360
Beef Kidney	350
Calf liver	420
Thymus	290
Brain	3100

Chicken: 75

Fish:

Caviar	300
Lobster	150
Oysters	150
Crab	150
Sole	50
Red perch	40
Mackerel	35
Cold fish	30

Milk + Milk products:

Whole milk (3.5% fat)	10
Skim milk	3
Double cream cheese (60-70% fat)	105
Fat cheese (45%)	90
Fat cheese (30%)	57
Low fat cheese (20%)	30
Low fat cheese (10%)	12
Ice cream	45

Fat:

Butter	280
Pork fat and other animal fats	100
Vegetable margarine	0

Eggs:

1 egg	280
Egg white	0
Egg yolk fresh (100g)	1400

Cholesterol and Associated Risk Factors

The answer to the problem of arteriosclerosis is essentially one of prevention. Take the time to find out your cholesterol baseline now. Never let your cholesterol level get too high. If some cholesterol plaques have formed in the arterial wall, there is still a good chance to get rid of them by normalizing your weight and eliminating cholesterol from your diet as much as possible. Lower total fat consumption by avoiding animal fats and by the use of vegetable oils and margarine. Quit smoking. If your blood pressure is elevated, get it under control. If diabetic or not, keep an optimal blood sugar level. One way to normalize your weight is to exercise regularly. Exercise, too, is helpful in both the sugar metabolism and the cholesterol metabolism. Up to the middle of your life, perhaps even up to 50 and 60, arteriosclerosis and its accompanying plaque formation is still a reversible disease, and can be positively influenced by a multifactorial approach.

Pointed Reminders

Loving wives should hang this notice about their stoves: "The way to a man's heart is (via his stomach) through his arteries." And the country's football training tables, traditionally laden with animal fats, should bear the device: "Cholesterol will block that pass...forever." Not only well-marbled steaks are rich in cholesterol. The most cholesterol-rich foods per ounce are the inner organs of animals and egg yolks *(Fig.11.)*. Three ounces of liver contain 300 mg. of cholesterol. Three ounces of brains contain 3000 mg., and one large egg yolk contains 300 mg. of cholesterol. The American Heart Association recommends decreasing the daily cholesterol intake from the present average 600 mg. per day to 300 mg. The only way to accomplish this is to choose low cholesterol foods like low fat milk products, fish, turkey and chicken, smaller and leaner meat portions and margarine. Skinned chicken and turkey, for example, contain only 60/70 mg. of cholesterol in a 3-oz. portion. Rather than face the autumn of your life sustained on carrot sticks and Granola, choose wisely NOW!

The Quality of Our Dietary Fat

And while you are choosing wisely, take into consideration the kind of quality of the fats you do eat. When we use the term fat quality we mean the effect a certain type of fat has on the blood cholesterol. Dietary fats are chemically determined in three classes as fatty acids. As we will learn, some dietary fatty acids tend to increase our blood cholesterol levels, some fatty acids have an influence on lowering cholesterol levels and, finally, another type of fatty acids is practically neutral towards the cholesterol levels, that

Fig. 12.

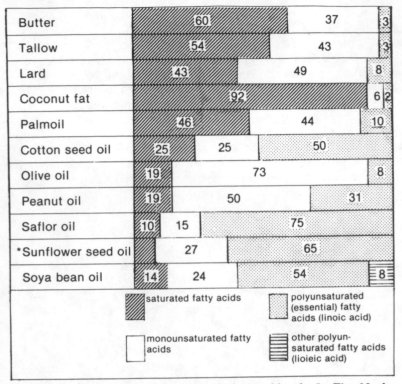

	saturated fatty acids		monounsaturated fatty acids		polyunsaturated (essential) fatty acids (linoic acid)		other polyunsaturated fatty acids (lioieic acid)
Butter	60		37		3		
Tallow	54		43		3		
Lard	43		49		8		
Coconut fat	92		6		2		
Palmoil	46		44		10		
Cotton seed oil	25		25		50		
Olive oil	19		73		8		
Peanut oil	19		50		31		
Saflor oil	10		15		75		
*Sunflower seed oil			27		65		
Soya bean oil	14		24		54		8

is, they do not increase or decrease cholesterol levels. In *Fig. 12.* the three kinds of fatty acids are presented: 1. predominantly saturated (primarily of animal origin); 2. predominantly polyunsaturated (many but not all vegetable oils); and 3. monounsaturated (peanut and olive oils). Saturated fatty acids increase cholesterol levels, while polyunsaturated fatty acids decrease cholesterol levels, and monounsaturated fatty acids neither raise nor lower these levels. As there is no good rule without its exception, a word to the wary—coconut and palm oils, although obviously stemming from vegetables, resemble animal fatty acids and increase blood cholesterol levels. On the other hand fish have a fatty acid composition similar to vegetable oils and decrease cholesterol levels. Exceptions are some seafoods like shrimp, prawns and caviar which are very high in cholesterol.

The evidence is in: cholesterol constricts and blocks your arteries, the vital highways to your heart. Remember, when you say you're just dying for some bacon and eggs and a cigarette—that is exactly what you are doing. You are also narrowing, along with your arteries, your chances for a long and healthy life.

*Corn oil is similar to sunflower seed oil with 10% saturated, 28% monounsaturated, and 53% polyunsaturated fatty acids. But it also contains 9% unlisted lipids.

4

Regular Exercise, Cardiovascular Fitness, and the Prevention of Coronary Heart Disease

R. Sanders Williams, M.D.

Fig. 13.
"Speaking generally, all parts of the body which have a function, if used in moderation and exercised in labors in which each is accustomed thereby become healthy, well developed and age more slowly; but if unused and left idle they become liable to disease, defective in growth and age quickly."

Hippocrates (n300 B.C.)

The idea that regular exercise promotes physical health, longevity, and a sense of well-being is by no means new. Statements attesting to the salutary effects of vigorous physical activity appear in the early Greek writings of Hippocrates and Plato, the teachings of the great Roman physician Galen, and in ancient Chinese religious doctrines (Fig. 13.). On the other hand, the situation where most members of a society, and not only a privileged few, have the luxury of making a conscious choice regarding the amount of exercise they perform is indeed a phenomenon limited to twentieth century industrialized nations such as the United States. Our rural ancestors encountered no such decision: the basic demands of everyday life required considerable physical effort.

In America today, not only are the physical demands of most jobs negligible, but substantial obstacles to exercise are programmed into our daily life routines. Urban communities based largely on transportation by personal automobile encourage families to live beyond walking distance of their place of work, school or shopping, and travel by foot or bicycle is generally unpleasant or unsafe along busy streets and highways.

It is clear that the path of least resistance for most Americans, and the path seemingly chosen by most, is a steady progression following the late teens into a largely sedentary existence. However, in increasing numbers, Americans are now choosing to spend some of their leisure hours in vigorous physical exercise such as jogging, cycling and swimming, making such activities a part of their daily routine. Since this decision represents a conscious choice for most, the question becomes "Why?": what benefits are motivating people to change their life habits? The most common answers are likely to be twofold: "I feel better when I exercise," and "regular exercise is going to help me be healthier and live longer". To some jogging enthusiasts, these answers may take on an almost religious significance (often to the extreme boredom of their friends and family), while to unyielding skeptics of the value of exercise, these answers serve only to enhance their belief that all joggers are afflicted with the rather advanced stages of mass hysteria. The remainder of this chapter is dedicated to those readers who, faced with the decision whether or not to exercise regularly, prefer to have the benefit of the evidence existing today regarding the effects of regular exercise upon the human body, and upon their risk for cardiovascular disease.

Effects of regular exercise

Several changes in important body processes become evident when an individual who has been inactive begins an exercise program, and some of the most striking changes involve the cardiovascular system; that is, the heart and blood vessels. The maximum pump ing capacity of the heart increases; the heart rate at rest and during levels of exercise short of one's maximum effort is slowed; and the length of time an individual can undergo any given level of exertion before fatiguing is increased. Blood pressure, if normal to start with, tends to be relatively unchanged, whereas blood pressure levels are generally reduced in persons with hypertension. To translate these effects into everyday life situations, an increased maximum pumping capacity of the heart means that after several months of regular exercise a person can perform harder levels of work before fatigue. Since the heart rate is the major feature determining the amount of oxygen required during exercise by the heart itself, a slower pulse rate at rest or at any given level of activity means that the activity can be performed at lower cardiac energy costs, with less "strain", so to speak, on the heart. It is primarily this latter effect that has led many cardiologists to prescribe supervised exercise programs to persons already afflicted with significant coronary artery disease. And finally, the value of an increased duration of exercise at any given workload before fatigue sets in is self-explanatory. With extreme levels of physical training such as performed by Olympic marathon runners or swimmers, the changes in heart rate and heart size become so striking that such persons are occasionally misclassified by physicians as "abnormal". Such extreme changes generally do not occur in adults who practice more modest exercise programs.

Together with these changes in cardiovascular function, several important alterations in body metabolism occur. The exercising muscles become more efficient in extracting oxygen from the blood, such that they can perform any given level of work with less blood flow required. In addition, the muscles become more proficient in utilizing the stores of body fat, as opposed to carbohydrates (sugars), as a source of metabolic fuel during exercise. With the increased caloric demands imposed by an exercise program, body weight tends to fall, and the percentage of body weight which exists as fat is reduced. Overweight persons trying to diet will lose weight more rapidly while exercising if they have the same food intake as while they were sedentary, while persons already at an ideal weight can eat more and still maintain their weight.

There are major changes in the forms of fat which circulate in the blood following a conditioning program as well. Cholesterol appears in human blood incorporated into two distinct types of particles: the low-density lipoprotein (LDL) and the high density lipoprotein (HDL). The levels of these two types of cholesterol-containing particles in the blood appear to have a great deal of importance in predicting one's risk of developing coronary heart disease. Cholesterol derived from LDL is incorporated into the walls of the arteries of the heart, and over a period of years this buildup can close off the artery and produce a heart attack or angina pectoris. The higher the level of circulating LDL in the blood, the greater the likelihood of developing coronary heart disease. The HDL form of cholesterol, however, appears to have a distinctly different effect. This particle may have the ability to actually remove cholesterol from the blood vessel walls, and in fact, the higher the levels of this form of cholesterol in the blood, the lower the risk of heart attack. Regular exercise, over a period of months, elevates the blood levels of HDL, the "good" form of cholesterol, and lowers the levels of LDL, the "bad" form of cholesterol. The other major form of blood fat, the triglycerides, also tend to be reduced by regular exercise. High levels of triglycerides, like LDL cholesterol, are associated with a higher risk for diseases of the blood vessels.

Recent research also indicates that regular exercise may affect the chemical systems which operate within the veins and arteries of the body to produce or dissolve blood clots. The formation of clots within blood vessels appears to be an important step in the disease processes which produce thrombophlebitis, pulmonary embolism, heart attack, and stroke. At least two effects of regular exercise that potentially could be beneficial in lowering the risk for such diseases have been described. Regular exercise appears to enhance fibrinolysis, the body's own chemical system for dissolving clots that are formed inside blood vessels. In addition, regular exercise may reduce the degree to which platelets (tiny corpuscles which circulate in the bloodstream, adhere to sites of damage on the inside of blood vessels, and are probably involved in the process of narrowing of the arteries of the heart) stick to one another or to blood vessel linings.

Regular exercise also improves the ability of the cells of the body to respond to insulin, the hormone released by the pancreas which, among several other effects, allows cells to utilize glucose. While this effect of exercise may be unimportant in normal thin persons, it achieves major significance in persons with diabetes, particularly the milder form of diabetes which appears largely in overweight adults. Such persons who require insulin injections or other medications for control of their blood sugar may be able to discontinue medications entirely and often have normal blood sugars following a program of physical conditioning.

To summarize, regular exercise has profound effects upon cardiovascular function and body metabolism. These changes allow an individual to perform harder activities without fatigue than were possible prior to an exercise program. In addition, the metabolic changes which occur with regular exercise significantly involve several of the most important risk factors for heart attack, with all the changes noted occurring in a favorable direction. Body weight, LDL cholesterol, and triglycerides are reduced, and HDL cholesterol is increased. Blood pressure, if abnormal, is generally lowered, and better control of blood sugar in diabetic persons is achieved.

Because of these important effects of regular exercise upon other established risk factors for heart attack, I think one can construct a simple pictorial model of current efforts in preventive cardiology (Fig. 14.). In this illustration, the goal of cardiovascular fitness is depicted as the rim of a wheel with habitual exercise shown as the hub. The other major risk factors can be conceived as the spokes emanating from this central hub. The model illustrates several important points: (1) exercise can have beneficial effects, direct or indirect, on all major known reversible risk factors for heart attack, and thus occupies a central place in preventive cardiology efforts; (2) however, the wheel won't turn without the spokes intact, and other modifications in dietary or smoking habits, in control of blood pressure or excessive psychological stress, must be coordinated with exercise for achieving the lowest possible risk.

Is there evidence that regular exercise in leisure time actually produces a lower incidence of heart attacks in exercising persons? Perhaps the best evidence to date comes from a study in which 17,000 college alumni responded to questionnaires regarding their physical activity. The results indicate that the risk of death from heart attack was significantly reduced in persons who habitually

Fig. 14.

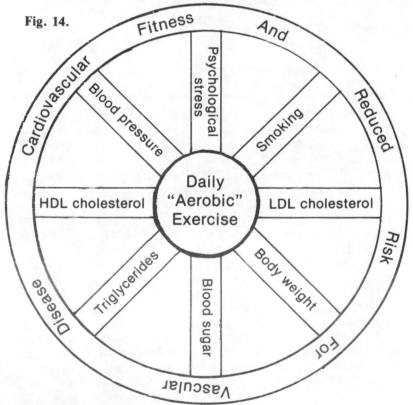

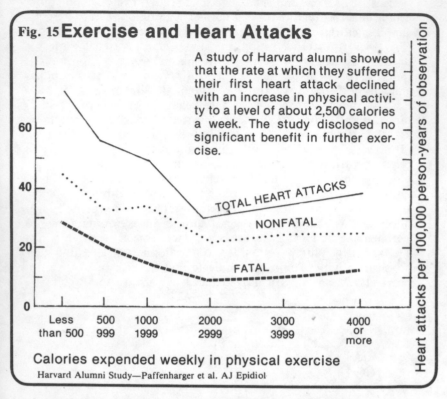

Fig. 15 Exercise and Heart Attacks

A study of Harvard alumni showed that the rate at which they suffered their first heart attack declined with an increase in physical activity to a level of about 2,500 calories a week. The study disclosed no significant benefit in further exercise.

TOTAL HEART ATTACKS

NONFATAL

FATAL

Calories expended weekly in physical exercise

Harvard Alumni Study—Paffenharger et al. AJ Epidiol

Heart attacks per 100,000 person-years of observation

burned 2000 to 2999 Kcal per week (about the energy consumed by jogging 25 miles) in vigorous exercise (Fig. 15.). Of interest is that this study showed no additional benefit of burning greater than 3000 Kcal per week. While further research is needed to confirm this finding, it suggests that rather modest exercise programs (jogging 4 miles a day for 5 days per week) may be all that is required to achieve maximal benefits upon risk for cardiovascular disease. (The apparently greater risk of persons consuming greater than 4000 Kcal/week over those consuming 2000-2999 Kcal was not statistically significant).

Other major studies of occupation-related exercise habits of San Francisco longshoremen and London transportation workers yielded similar conclusions: the more physically active persons experienced a significantly lower risk of death from heart attack. Further research is needed to amplify and confirm these results, but the weight of the scientific evidence available to us today suggests that regular exercise does indeed have an important role in reducing one's risk for cardiovascular disease. The person who exercises because "exercise is going to help me be healthier and live longer" is probably right. Furthermore, it is important to note that, whereas the effects of regular exercise upon longevity remain controversial in the scientific and medical literature, the effects of physical conditioning upon functional work capacity, the "I feel better when I exercise" response mentioned previously, are widely accepted.

Practical pointers and common questions
The preceding paragraphs have dealt with the question "Why should I exercise?" The next important query is "How do I exercise?"

What kind of exercise is best?
To produce the cardiovascular and metabolic effects described earlier, one must perform "aerobic" exercise involving the repeated "dynamic" use of major muscle groups over a sustained period of time. The term "aerobic" means "oxygen-requiring" and should be contrasted to "anaerobic" forms of exercise which are performed without the requirement for delivery of oxygen to the exercising muscles. When you walk or jog at a comfortable pace for a half-hour, your muscles' energy needs are being met "aerobically" by the continuous supply of oxygen and nutrients provided by the bloodstream. If you walk or jog faster, the heart's pumping ability and the ability of your muscles to extract the supply of oxygen they need from the blood can keep up with the increased energy demands for a while, but only until a certain limit, called the "anaerobic threshold", is reached. When muscular work exceeds this limit, the exercising muscles must rely on a very small supply of nutrients which are already present within the muscle in order to keep working. Since this "anaerobic" (meaning "without oxygen") work is much less biochemically efficient, the supply of muscle nutrients is rapidly exhausted, and you tire quickly. This phenomenon explains why most persons can walk comfortably for long periods of time, but rapidly become exhausted when attempting much harder work, like running up stairs. In addition, anaerobic work produces lactic acid, the accumulation of which impairs muscle function, producing fatigue or even pain. During anaerobic work the lungs and heart must also work much harder in order to expire the extra carbon dioxide which is produced, and a sensation of breathlessness is encountered. These events during anaerobic exercise are in distinct contrast to the situation during aerobic exercise, when the heart and lungs increase their function smoothly and gradually, with the oxygen needs of the working muscle being met by increased blood flow. Aerobic exercise should not be uncomfortable, and can be sustained quite readily for long periods of time. Anaerobic work is necessary for the Olympic sprinter or for a football halfback, but is often uncomfortable and

is not the form of exercise which most readily produces cardiovascular fitness.

The term "dynamic" exercise refers to activities such as walking, jogging, cycling, or swimming wherein the muscles involved are in rather continuous motion. This is to be contrasted with "static" forms of exercise that often involve straining against a resistance with little motion and include weight lifting and water skiing. These latter forms of exercise may be enjoyable or may be useful for other goals such as building muscle size and strength, but they do little to improve overall cardiovascular function and do not produce the beneficial effects upon cardiovascular risk factors which occur with regular "dynamic" or "aerobic" exercise.

Sports activities such as golf, tennis (particularly doubles), football, baseball, bowling or motor sports do not generally produce the desired cardiovascular effects, primarily because the exercise is either not intense enough, not continuous enough, or involves sudden bursts of extreme effort ("anaerobic" work) rather than steady rhythmic activity. Other recreational activities like gardening, lawn care, or light carpentry have the same limitations. Certain other sports like cross-country skiing, soccer, full-court basketball, rowing, squash, or "aerobic" dance usually meet the requirements for producing cardiovascular fitness, but for most persons the activities mentioned above — walking, jogging, cycling, or swimming —are most easily incorporated into their daily routines. Among these four activities, there is little inherent advantage of one over the other, and one may choose the form of exercise most suitable to one's preferences. Walking or jogging require no special equipment other than proper footgear, are not limited to any particular hours of the day, can be performed alone, often in one's neighborhood so there is no need for transportation to a special facility. They are thus more easily incorporated into a busy daily schedule. Cycling on a stationary ergometer or swimming in indoor pool facilities, on the other hand, are not limited by darkness or inclement weather. The most important point is that, whichever form of aerobic exercise one chooses, it must be performed regularly and become part of one's daily routine.

How much exercise is enough?
Continuous aerobic exercise for 30 minutes, three times per week is probably the minimum level of activity sufficient to produce a cardiovascular conditioning effect. In addition, the exercise during this 30 minute session must be intense enough to raise the body's oxygen demands to at least 60% of one's maximum oxygen consumption. Furthermore, it is not necessary for the exercise to be exhaustive for the conditioning effects to occur. In general, exercise at intensities greater than 85% of one's maximum oxygen consumption cannot be sustained for the periods of time necessary for

proper cardiovascular training, and should be avoided.

Exercise physiologists can monitor exercise to estimate the amount of oxygen being consumed by measuring the rate of the heart beat during exercise. While more accurate, though more complex, formulas exist, 60%-85% of maximum oxygen consumption will occur at heart rates around 75%-85% of one's maximal heart rate. Since an individual's maximum heart rate can be approximated by another simple calculation (maximum heart rate (beats/min) = 220 minus age), it is relatively easy to use the pulse rate as a way to determine the adequacy of the intensity of an aerobic exercise session. For example, a forty-year-old man should elevate his heart rate to between 135 and 153 beats/min during exercise (220 - 40 x 75% = 135) to produce the desired effects on cardiovascular fitness. While it is relatively easy to learn to count one's own heart rate from the radial (wrist) pulse, another simple rule of thumb can be applied: during exercise, one should have a sense of breathing faster, and more deeply, yet still be able to carry on a conversation without breathlessness. This level of exercise during a jogging or cycling session will probably fall in the desired range.

To further illustrate this point regarding heart rate during exercise, consider the example of a healthy, but overweight and sedentary forty-year-old man who begins an exercise program. At the outset, walking at the relatively slow pace (on level ground) of 1 mile every 20 minutes, he would probably achieve a heart rate of 140 beats per minute, well withing his training range. With time, as his level of fitness improved he would have to walk more briskly, at 1 mile per 15 minutes for example, to achieve this same heart rate. With still more time, he would have to begin to jog, perhaps at around 1 mile per 12 minutes to reach a rate of 140. If he achieved superb conditioning, he could run at rates of 6 to 7 minutes per mile, still at the same heart rate of 140. Obviously, with improved conditioning and faster rates he would go farther (and burn more calories) during his 30 minute workout: from 1.5 miles at his initial rate of 1 mile every 20 minutes, to 4.3 miles if he achieved the rapid speed of 1 mile every seven minutes.

I have defined the minimal level of exercise sufficient to induce a cardiovascular conditioning effect. But what is the optimal level? What amount of exercise is required to maximize the apparently beneficial effects of habitual physical activity upon risk for vascular disease? The answer is not entirely clear, but the available evidence suggests that levels of activity somewhat greater than 30 min. three times a week confer greater protective effects. In the previously mentioned study of college alumni, the minimal risk of death from heart attack was noted in the group who consumed 2000-2999 Kcal per week of vigorous activity, the energy required to walk or jog 20 to 30 miles. For a jogger who runs at a pace of nine minutes per mile, 36 minutes of jogging, five times per week would add up to 20 miles per week. It may also be important to increase one's level of physical activity outside of the time specifically devoted to the daily exercise session. Climbing stairs instead of riding the elevator, and walking on short trips instead of using an automobile or public transportation are highly recommended.

Can vigorous exercise be dangerous?

Yes. Serious medical problems, including sudden death, can occur during strenuous exercise in persons with certain cardiovascular diseases. Some conditions, like severe hypertension, coronary artery disease, aortic stenosis, or an entity called hypertrophic cardiomyopathy may produce no symptoms in sedentary persons, yet lead to life-threatening problems during a sudden bout of vigorous exercise. Smokers who inhale tobacco smoke immediately following an unaccustomed bout of exercise (like climbing stairs at a football stadium) may be at special risk if they have unrecognized heart disease. Exercise can be highly beneficial to persons with coronary artery disease or hypertension but must be carefully controlled, and should be recommended only under the close supervision of a physician. For this reason, it is essential that all persons contemplating a major change in their exercise habits consult their physician and undergo a thorough medical history and physical examination prior to beginning an exercise program. In certain cases an exercise stress test or other cardiac diagnostic procedures should be performed in addition to the physical examination.

Joggers unquestionably suffer an increased risk of orthopedic injuries, though these are generally minor and self-limited. There is no current evidence that running induces a greater risk of degenerative arthritis in later life. In fact, habitual physical activity has been shown to delay the rate of calcium loss from bone which usually occurs with the aging process, particularly in women, and which produces the propensity to fractures of the hip and spine noted in the elderly. The risk of foot, ankle, knee, and hip injuries noted in joggers can probably be lessened by wearing proper footgear (reasonable advice is available from reputable sporting goods stores) and by avoiding sudden changes in the training program in terms of mileage, speed, or running surface. The risk of orthopedic injuries is considerably less during aerobic activities such as swimming or cycling than during jogging.

Summary

To summarize, regular physical activity is clearly associated with improved cardiovascular performance, and with beneficial changes in major risk factors for cardiovascular disease. Furthermore, the available evidence strongly supports the contention that these changes are indeed associated with a lowered risk of death from cardiovascular disease, the leading killer of Americans today. The following recommendations have been presented:

(1) Consult your physician before beginning an exercise program.

(2) The types of exercise producing beneficial cardiovascular effects include walking/jogging, cycling, swimming and other selected sports activities which were previously listed. Many recreational sports activities practiced in this country today, though beneficial or enjoyable for other reasons, do not produce the desired effects upon the heart and circulation.

(3) The aerobic exercise sessions should include at least 30 minutes of continuous activity at intensities sufficient to elevate the heart rate to a range of 75-85% of the maximal heart rate, and should be performed at least three, but preferably five, times weekly.

(4) Physical activity should be increased, whenever possible, at times other than the designated exercise sessions. Stair-climbing and walking are recommended over motorized transportation.

(5) Modern concepts regarding the prevention of heart attack emphasize the need for proper diet, cessation of smoking, control of high blood pressure, and modification of high-stress lifestyles, in addition to an aerobic exercise program.

5

Hypertension

Siegfried Heyden, M.D.
William DeMaria, M.D.

Introduction

Hypertension or high blood pressure is the most common chronic disease affecting the American people. An estimated 35 million Americans suffer with significant hypertension while another 25 million adults have borderline hypertension. Hypertension is *the* important factor contributing to 500,000 cases of stroke each year resulting in 175,000 deaths. It is one of the main factors in the 1,250,000 heart attacks that occur each year.

The disease can exist for 15 or 20 years without signs or symptoms. Neither headaches nor nose bleeds, dizziness or black spots in front of the eyes are present in hypertension during the first two decades. As a result, a large number of these afflicted people are unaware of the elevation of their blood pressure. Thus, the need for annual checkups is quite clear.

Early recognition has taken on even more urgency in view of results from recent international studies of hypertension. The studies indicate that the earlier the hypertensive person received adequate management of this condition, the more likely one can prevent some of its serious complications.

The three major complications of hypertension are stroke, heart attack, and kidney failure. The underlying factor causing these three major complications of longstanding untreated hypertension, is decreased or complete blockage of blood flow through the arteries. This blockage usually arises from varying degrees of atherosclerosis (hardening of the arteries) which is much accelerated by the increased pressure inside the arteries. Of less dramatic but of considerable impact is the increased susceptibility of hypertensive patients to additional organ and systems diseases. Because hypertension involves the blood vessels throughout the human body, it is thus to be expected that all parts of the body, for example, respiratory and gastrointestinal tracts, are subject to changes associated with this long-standing disease.

Evidence to this effect came from two long-term population studies in Framingham, Massachusetts, and in Evans County, Georgia. The longest treatment study, a five year intervention study involving 10,000 hypertensives in 14 centers across the United States, revealed that intensive medication therapy reduced the mortality from not only heart and blood vessel diseases but from all causes. These observations document further the need for early recognition and proper care of all persons with hypertension.

How the Blood Pressure Is Measured
It is important to use an appropriately sized cuff when determining the blood pressure. Persons with fat arms whose blood

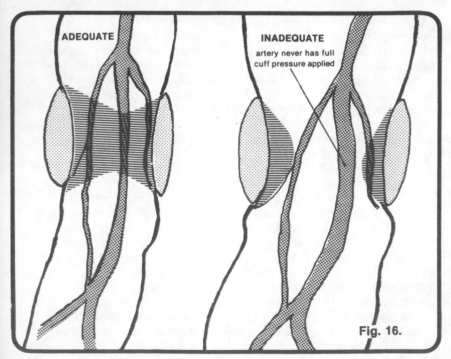

ADEQUATE

INADEQUATE

artery never has full cuff pressure applied

Fig. 16.

pressure is taken with an undersized cuff can be recorded as having falsely high levels of blood pressure. How the blood pressure measurement is done correctly in the normal arm and inadequately in the fat arm is demonstrated in the picture. With air pumped into the regular blood pressure cuff, the main arm artery is compressed. As soon as the air pressure is released by opening a valve at the cuff, the blood flows through the artery with every pulse wave. The first wave going through becomes the first audible sound heard when listening with a stethoscope over the artery. This first sound is called the upper or systolic blood pressure. After a few seconds, the blood flows evenly through the artery. With this even flow, the sound of the pulse disappears. The mercury scale is watched closely at that moment, and we call this reading the diastolic or lower blood pressure level.

On the right side of the picture the arm is much too big to obtain an accurate measurement using a regular size cuff. A wider and longer cuff size is necessary to properly compress the artery and only then would we be able to accurately measure the blood pressure. In a normal arm, as noted on the left, the pressure is measured correctly because the main artery can be readily compressed.

Blood pressure measurement thus provides us with two different figures. A person with a systolic reading under 140 mm Hg and diastolic under 90 mm Hg is considered normotensive. Borderline hypertension is defined with systolic figures between 140 and 159, and diastolic between 90 and 94. Significant hypertension is defined by the World Health Organization as a systolic blood pressure above 160 and diastolic blood pressure above 95 mm Hg.

In addition to using the appropriately sized cuff, it is also important to position the arm so that the physician or nurse listens to the arterial sound *at the heart level*. This is equally important whether sitting, standing, or reclining. If the arm is lowered below the level of the heart, a falsely elevated blood pressure may be recorded.

Normally, a blood pressure is lowest when lying down and is slightly higher while standing and walking and more elevated during physical activity such as climbing stairs.

Causes of Hypertension: Family History, Obesity, Salt

Factors which influence development of this disease are a positive family history of high blood pressure, overweight and excess table salt (Sodium Chloride) intake. Other factors can *temporarily* affect the blood pressure. Cigarette smoking and psychological stress are two such examples.

Surveys reveal that 60 percent of hypertensive patients are moderately to severely overweight. In addition, average Americans eat in excess of 15 grams of table salt each day. Healthy adults normally require less than 1 gram of salt each day.

The typical patient is a man or a woman in their fifties, with moderate to marked overweight who usually responds well to weight loss with a reduction in blood pressure. If, in addition to obesity, a family history of hypertension or stroke is present, this weight loss becomes even more important. But it is not the weight reduction alone that matters. Weight reducing diets are almost automatically low in sodium salt and this is probably the main reason that weight loss helps in reducing the elevated blood pressure.

We have followed a group of ten hypertensive patients all of whom were overweight. Their weight loss varied from as little as 20 pounds to as much as 180 pounds. However, all of them normalized their blood pressure levels because they used a salt restricted diet. The favorable response of the blood pressure to weight loss may be expected within a few weeks. It is mandatory, therefore, for those patients already on drug therapy to take blood pressure measurements regularly during weight reduction. Otherwise, the pressure may drop to such a low level that the patient experiences symptoms of dizziness or fainting spells.

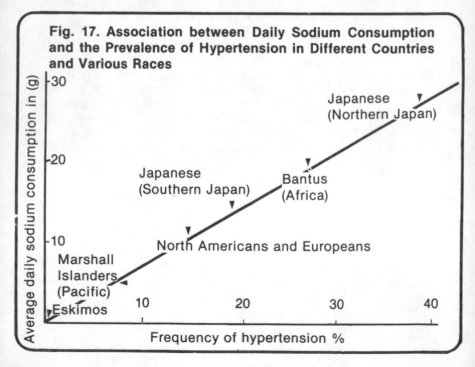

Fig. 17. Association between Daily Sodium Consumption and the Prevalence of Hypertension in Different Countries and Various Races

The Role of Sodium Salt

There is a lot of naturally occurring salt in commonly eaten foods such as milk, milk products, meat and bread. In addition, prepared and canned foods usually have an excess amount of salt added. This requires the hypertensive person to be very cautious of the foods he/she eats and to read the labels for the sodium content. A low salt diet necessitates the elimination of salting during the preparation of foods and no salt addition to the foods at the time of eating.

As will be mentioned later in the chapter on treatment of obesity, overweight persons also have a water retention problem. Salt retains fluid in every cell of the body. Thus to rid the body of this excess fluid requires a marked reduction in the salt intake. Salting at the table is an acquired habit which begins in early childhood and persists throughout adulthood. Experiments have shown that the acquired taste for salt is much more prevalent among hypertensive patients than among normotensive persons.

Fig. 17. demonstrates the correlation between hypertension and daily salt intake in different parts of the world. The average salt intake or sodium consumption among Eskimos is said to be the lowest in the world. They rarely develop hypertension. Marshall Islanders consume very little salt. In addition, they use potassium ashes for spicing their food. The frequency of high blood pressure is only about 5 percent. In contrast, Europeans and North Americans use an average of 15 grams of table salt or sodium chloride per day which equals about three teaspoons of salt (1 teaspoon = 5g NaCl). Between 15 and 20 percent of adults suffer from hypertension. In southern Japan salt intake is much higher, due in large measure to the almost daily eaten salted fish. The average sodium chloride intake is estimated to be 20 grams. Between 20 and 25% of these southern Japanese adults have hypertension. Bantus in South Africa consume around 25 grams of sodium chloride and the frequency of hypertension among that population was found to be 30 per cent. The highest recorded sodium chloride intake is observed in people of northern Japan where 30 to 35 grams of sodium chloride are consumed daily. The frequency of hypertension is 40 percent in this adult population. Therefore, an impressive correlation between salt intake and frequency of hypertension points to the importance of salt restriction both in prevention and treatment of hypertension.

Unfortunately, it is not easy to recognize all the "hidden" sources of salt. For example, Alka Seltzer, commonly used for stomach distress, has a high salt content and a cup of bouillon contains an excessive amount of salt.

The Role of Potassium Salt:
It is most important to note what happens to both Sodium (Na) and Potassium (K) salt content during food processing as exemplified in this Table. (Please note in the Table the chemical abbreviation for sodium is Na and the abbreviation for potassium is K.) In the fresh produce, 3 ounces (100 grams) of peas contain almost no sodium but a significant amount (380 mg.) of potassium. In frozen peas, during blanching, when done commercially, the sodium content is increased to 100 mg. and the potassium is reduced from the original 380 to 160 mg. In canned peas, where salt is always added for preservation, we see a further increase of the sodium content to 230, whereas the potassium content remains reduced. The table demonstrates the tremendous alterations of these salts as we change from fresh to canned produce. High sodium is present in most canned products, particularly soups, vegetables and meats.

Fig.18.

Fresh Produce (3 oz)	Na (mg)	K (mg)
Green Beans (fresh)	1.7	256
canned	236	95
Carrots (Fresh)	50	311
canned	236	110
Asparagus (fresh)	2	240
canned	236	166
Spinach (fresh)	62	662
canned	320	260
Peas (fresh)	0.9	380
canned	230	180

A relatively new aspect of hypertension is a closer look at the effects of low potassium (K) intake in hypertensive patients. It is thought that low K intake may be an important additive to the growing list of factors which contribute to the origin or further elevation of high blood pressure. Some of these interesting observations have been made especially as regards K intake among blacks when compared with whites.

A comparison of the potassium intake between blacks and whites living in Evans County, Georgia; in Washington, D.C.; Jackson,

Mississippi; and New Orleans, Louisiana, shows that the intake of potassium is approximately 50 percent lower in blacks than in whites for two reasons.

1. Black people, particularly in rural areas, often cook their foods for several hours. Potassium is located inside the cells of the meat and vegetables. With prolonged cooking, the potassium is released into the cooking water which is subsequently discarded. As a result, the potassium is not available for eating.

2. Black people, because of both tradition and reasons of expense, eat less potassium containing foods, such as fresh fruits and salads.

At present we believe a low potassium intake coupled with a high sodium intake enhance the likelihood of developing hypertension. This may account, in part, for the higher rate of hypertension noted in our black population.

Fruits, vegetables and salads are high in potassium. In a well balanced diet recommended in the primary prevention of high blood pressure, one should consume at least two fruits and two vegetables each day. In addition, chicken, turkey, lean hamburger and fish are relatively high in potassium. The daily minimum requirement is 2500 mg. K per day according to the McGovern Report. Cantaloupes, oranges, grapefruits, watermelons, and bananas are rich sources of potassium, and most of these foods are also low in calories.

An ideal intake to supply well over 2500 mg. K (i.e., twice as much) would be half a cantaloupe for breakfast (880 mg.), and one glass of grapefruit juice (380 mg.); a salad for lunch, consisting of two tomatoes (680 mg.), and a turkey sandwich (4 oz. = 350 mg.); and a fish dinner, e.g. with 9 oz. of trout (1410 mg. - each 3 oz. = 470 mg.), one medium baked potato (410 mg.) and 3 oz. of Brussel Sprouts (300 mg.), with 2 cups of fresh strawberries for dessert (540 mg.).

Potassium and Diuretics

It should be mentioned, however, that a patient who is taking water tablets (diuretics) to lower blood pressure levels would not benefit as much from such a K-rich diet. This is due to the action of diuretics which causes increased urinary excretion of potassium, sodium *and chloride.* All the potassium-rich foods contain little or no chlorides. If the body is deprived of chlorides such as through diuretic action, the increased intake of potassium-rich foods is of no avail. The potassium can stay in the body only when bound to chlorides. Hypertensive patients on diuretic medication who may experience a lowering of their potassium blood levels, need to take the drug potassium chloride (K Cl) in tablet or liquid form. On the other hand, a person not taking diuretics, will always have plenty of chlorides in circulation and therefore, the potassium from the food intake will find enough chloride to associate with.

Elevated Blood Pressure in the Young
Emphasis on low sodium and high potassium foods is recommended for children because it is in the young people where we have the best chances to prevent the development of high blood pressure.

Although hypertension is more common in adults, it does occur in children. A study was done of 30 young persons between 15 and 19 years of age who had normal blood pressure levels, namely, below 110 systolic and below 70 diastolic in 1960. In 1968 when they were reexamined, four of them had slightly elevated blood pressure levels, but all remained in good health.

A contrasting study was done of a group of 30 youngsters who in 1960 had elevated blood pressure levels of 140/90 and higher. In 1968, after seven years of observation, the consequences of long-term, untreated high blood pressure in young persons were noted. Eleven of the 30 adolescents have severe problems in the blood vessels of the heart and brain. Two of the girls died of strokes during pregnancy. A group of seven boys and girls with an initially high blood pressure who subsequently became borderline hypertensive, remained in good health. Of considerable interest is the group of 12 adolescents whose blood pressures returned to normal levels although no treatment was provided for them.

Upon review of the records of these 30 adolescents we noted one consistent factor which probably accounts for the dramatic differences in outcome. That factor was their body weight. These teenagers who are no longer healthy gained an average of 27 pounds over the seven-year period, whereas those adolescents whose blood pressure returned to normal without treatment either were normal weight and remained weight stable or lost weight if they were initially overweight. This study emphasizes the importance of high blood pressure which occurs in about 5 percent of our teenagers and demonstrates the urgent need for weight control as the most promising action in the prevention of adolescent hypertension.

Hypertension and Stroke
As was just demonstrated in the unfortunate fate of the two young hypertensive females with strokes, a most important target organ of hypertension is the brain. There is a certain order of risk factors for stroke, namely, high blood pressure, obesity, and high blood sugar. We noted earlier from a recent nationwide survey that 60 percent of hypertensive patients are moderately to severely obese. Again, our first line of defense *against* hypertension should be normalization of weight.

Hypertension and Heart Attacks
The heart is another major target of hypertension, especially in the adult. The untreated hypertensive pressure damages the two

major blood vessels called coronary arteries (see Fig. 6, page 34).

The normal artery is wide open, allowing the red blood cells to flow freely through the blood vessel. These red blood cells carry oxygen which is essential for normal function of the heart muscle. In a person who has had elevated and untreated blood pressure for 20 or 30 years, one may expect an advanced stage of a deforming process in the coronary artery. The hypertensive patient accumulates deposits of fat substances in the wall of the blood vessel. This fact and the constant high pressure inside the blood vessel causes thickening of the arterial wall and subsequently narrows the opening of the artery to the extent that decreasing numbers of red blood cells are able to pass through. Thus, hardening of the artery, or atherosclerosis, eventually deprives the heart muscle of its oxygen. If a small blood clot gets caught in such a narrowed segment of the artery, the blood flow would stop completely and abruptly. That is what happens in a heart attack. No more oxygen can be delivered to this part of the heart because no more red blood cells can pass through the vessel.

When the blood supply to the heart muscle stops, severe chest pain usually occurs and is described by most patients as excruciating, often radiating from the left chest into the left arm. One-third of all patients with their first heart attack die from sudden death and the other 60 percent survive and usually form a scar in the heart muscle within two weeks.

As the blood pressure continues to rise, there is an increasing danger of heart attacks occurring. The danger of heart attacks doubles if the hypertensive patient also smokes cigarettes. Again we state the urgent need for vigorous, continuous and early treatment of the person diagnosed as having hypertension.

Conclusion

In summary, optimal management of hypertension requires close and continuing attention to the following:

(1) Weight control. If overweight one would be advised to lose between 20 and 40 pounds.

(2) Restrict salt to 5 grams per day. Do not use the salt shaker and no salting in the preparation of food in the kitchen.

(3) Increase use of herbs and spices. Avoid high salt containing foods such as ham, pretzels, bouillon cubes and pickles.

(4) Use of drugs when indicated by your physician. The goal is to keep the diastolic blood pressure at or below 85 mm Hg.

(5) No smoking (although there is nothing wrong with an occasional cigar).

(6) Regular exercise as advised by your doctor.

(7) Blood pressure measurement every month after normalization and a check-up by your physician or nurse every four months thereafter.

6

Stress

James A. Blumenthal, Ph.D.

Poets, philosophers, and scientists have long been conscious of the relationship between stress and the heart. The heart leaps for joy, breaks with grief, throbs in love and stops in terror. It is the heart that binds and unifies the mind and body. Stress is part of our everyday language, and virtually everyone "knows" what it is.

The relationship between stress and illness has also received growing attention. The past half century has witnessed a health revolution in the United States: sickness and death are no longer related to the infectious diseases that plagued Americans at the turn of the century; rather, they are related to chronic diseases—heart attack, stroke, and cancer—all of which are thought to be related to stress.

Walter B. Cannon, a noted physiologist, was one of the first scientists to apply the concept of stress to physical health. The term "stress" was borrowed from the field of engineering, in which it referred to an external force directed at some physical object. The resultant "strain" referred to the temporary change in the structure of the object. For example, a heavy truck crossing a wooden bridge causes a realignment in the structure of the bridge (strain) as it gives under the weight of the truck (stress). Similarly, a psychological stress may be the loss of a loved one, a financial setback or a change in health. The results of these events would be the subsequent psychological and physiological adjustments such as feelings of depression, anxiety and disturbed appetite or sleep patterns.

Cannon was especially interested in emergency reactions; that is, the body's response to potentially life-threatening situations. In one experiment, he carefully studied the reactions of a cat that was suddenly exposed to a dog. He noted a variety of changes: the cat's circulation speeded up; there was increased blood sugar for quick energy and blood clotting mechanisms were accelerated in case of injury and loss of blood; breathing became faster and the cat was alert and attentive. These changes were actually highly adaptive; they represented an integrated set of responses that prepared the animal for vigorous muscular activity involved in attacking or avoiding the dangerous situation. Hence Cannon coined the term "fight or flight response" as a basic adaptational reaction to emergency situations. He noted that a variety of situations could elicit this response pattern including physical situations (e.g., physical injury, excessive heat, lack of food or water) and psychological or emotional upset. These kinds of situations will be discussed later in this chapter.

There have been hundreds of scientific studies on stress since Cannon's pioneering work. While it is beyond the scope of this brief overview to cite these studies, suffice it to say that research on stress falls into three broad categories: (1) studies of the person; (2) studies of situations; and (3) studies of the interaction of the person and situation. Let us consider each briefly:

1. The Person
A major element in our understanding of stress is that it involves a subjective feeling of some kind. Anxiety, frustration, fear—all are often used synonymously for "stress." More accurately, these feelings represent the phenomenology or experience of stress.

Similarly, stress results in very dramatic changes in physical, as well as psychological, characteristics. These physiological alterations include (a) circulatory changes: increased systolic blood pressure, heart rate, pulse pressure and increased blood flow to skeletal muscles, heart, lungs and brain; (b) exocrine changes in the skin: increased sweating and skin conductance (e.g., cold, clammy hands); (c) respiratory changes: increased rate of respiration; (d) gastrointestinal changes: decreased gastric motility and activity; and (e) metabolic changes: increased levels of free fatty acids, sugar, and lactic acid.

Hans Selye, an endocrinologist, extended Cannon's work, and specified mechanisms within the person that are, in effect, responses to external stimuli. He termed these specific stimuli *stressors* since they elicited a particular biological reaction that had both short term and long term effects. Selye views stress as an *adaptational* response—an organized set of biologic reactions that help prevent bodily damage. However, he believes that these adaptational processes, particularly when prolonged, can actually produce injury, and ultimately death. For example, Selye believes that the chronic outpouring of adrenalin (a hormone that affects the body's metabolism) or persistent elevations of heart rate and blood pressure could actually damage the body's tissues and organs, including the heart itself. While the initial set of responses are viewed as healthy adjustments to potentially dangerous events, over long periods of time the body's reaction may become harmful. We also now recognize that external stimuli are not the only stressors, but also internal events (conscious and unconscious thoughts and feelings) can serve as very potent stressors. For example, chronic worry—anticipating problems at every turn—can produce chronic arousal in which blood pressure and heart rate are persistently elevated.

2. The situation
Evidence is also accumulating that stressful life events are likely to be followed by a wide variety of illnesses, including everything from heart disease to the common cold. Thomas Holmes and Richard Rahe initially studied the relationship between various life changes and the health status of over 5,000 individuals. From their early investigations they derived a list of forty-three life events that appeared to precede the onset of various diseases. The list is shown in Fig. 19.

As you can see, each event (e.g., divorce, marriage, change in residence) is assigned a specific score or weight. Scores for all individuals were totaled and it was discovered that the higher the level of life change scores, the greater the likelihood of developing physical illness.

Only thirty percent of those who had low life change scores (that is, relatively few life change events) suffered some form of sickness or physical ailment within a two-year period, as compared to fifty percent of those who had moderate life change scores and eighty percent of those with high levels of life change. Thus, it was demonstrated that life change is a significant form of stress that is related to greater chances of becoming sick.

In contrast, a situational characteristic that appears to have positive value is the presence of social supports in the individual's environment. *Social support* is are defined as a situation in which the individual feels that he or she

    a. is loved or cared for
    b. is esteemed or valued by other individuals or groups
    c. belongs to a network of communication and mutual obligation.

Research has shown, quite convincingly, that people who have high levels of social support do not develop illnesses as serious as

Fig. 19. Social Readjustment Rating Scale

Rank	Life event	Mean value
1	Death of Spouse	100
2	Divorce	73
3	Marital separation	65
4	Jail term	63
5	Death of close family member	63
6	Personal injury or illness	53
7	Marriage	50
8	Fired at work	47
9	Marital reconciliation	45
10	Retirement	45
11	Change in health of family member	44
12	Pregnancy	40
13	Sex difficulties	39
14	Gain of new family member	39
15	Business readjustment	39
16	Change in financial state	38
17	Death of close friend	37
18	Change to different line of work	36
19	Change in number of arguments with spouse	35
20	Mortgage over $10,000	31
21	Foreclosure of mortgage or loan	30
22	Change in responsibilites at work	29
23	Son or daughter leaving home	29
24	Trouble with in-laws	29
25	Outstanding personal achievement	28
26	Wife begin or stop work	26
27	Begin or end school	26
28	Change in living conditions	25
29	Revision of personal habits	24
30	Trouble with boss	23
31	Change in work hours or conditions	20
32	Change in residence	20
33	Change in schools	20
34	Change in recreation	19
35	Change in church activities	19
36	Change in social activities	18
37	Mortgage or loan less than $10,000	17
38	Change in sleeping habits	16
39	Change in number of family get-togethers	15
40	Change in eating habits	15
41	Vacation	13
42	Christmas	12
43	Minor violations of the law	11

From Holmes, T.H. and Rahe, R.H.J. Psychosom Res. 11:216, 1967 those who lack social supports. That is, people with families, friends, and colleagues seem to be relatively protected from the potentially deleterious effects of the life changes listed in Table 1.

Our twentieth century industrialized society has created a stressful environment that is difficult to avoid. Long lines of traffic, crowded living conditions, excessive uncontrollable noise, smog—all bombard and insult our sensibilities. James Henry at UCLA Medical Center performed an interesting series of experiments using mice as his subjects. He kept his mice in crowded living conditions that closely resemble our urban cities. The mice had to compete for space, and experienced extreme crowding. Not surprisingly, these poor mice were soon discovered to exhibit sustained elevations of blood pressure. In effect, they developed hypertension. Situations make a difference in how we feel and how our bodies function. Certain environments can create harmful psychological and physical effects, while others can actually promote good health.

Scientists often study the effects of stress on animals. These may be referred to as *analogue* studies since they simulate the effects of stress on humans. One of the best known experiments is Brady's study of "executive monkeys." When monkeys were trained to press a bar to avoid a painful electric shock, they soon developed bleeding ulcers and subsequently died. In contrast, yoked control monkeys—that is, monkeys who received the same number of shocks but who did not have to learn when to press the bar—did not develop ulcers. In a later experiment, rats were trained to press a bar but could avoid the shock by pressing the bar before a warning light went off. In this experiment, the "executive" rats, those who were in a position to effect the administration of shock, did not develop ulcers; however, their yoked control counterparts did develop the ulcers! While these experiments appear somewhat contradictory, the implication is that it is important to have a sense of control over the environment, combined with feedback as to the effectiveness of the behavior. Effective behavior increases feelings of competence and expectations of success, and may enhance physical well-being.

The relationship between stress and the success of performance is defined by the so-called Yerkes-Dodson Law. Simply put, there is an interaction between the level of stress and the nature of the task. This can be seen in Fig. 20.

That is to say for any given task, there is an optimal level of arousal at which performance will be most effective. This optimal intensity of arousal is dependent on the complexity of the task. For easy or routine tasks, such as performing simple arithmetic problems (e.g., calculate 7 + 12), moderate levels of arousal would enhance performance. However, performance on complex or difficult tasks (e.g., calculate 117 x 434) would be disrupted by ex-

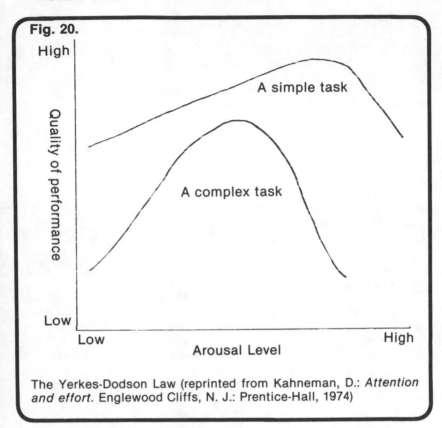

Fig. 20.

The Yerkes-Dodson Law (reprinted from Kahneman, D.: *Attention and effort.* Englewood Cliffs, N. J.: Prentice-Hall, 1974)

cessive levels of arousal.

The Yerkes-Dodson relationsip provides scientific evidence for what we know from our experience: a little stress is good for us and actually helps us perform better on certain tasks. However, beyond a certain point, stress causes excessive arousal and actually interferes with our performance especially on difficult or complex tasks. In general, moderate levels of arousal seem to be most helpful, while extreme levels are unpleasant and disruptive. Some people may actually seek out stimulation and enjoy the feeling of arousal accompanying such behaviors as driving fast automobiles, watching a boxing match, or skiing down a mountain. Being in *control* of the situation is very important. Uncontrollability of the situation gives rise to feelings of helplessness and hopelessness. These negative emotions can cause a decline in performance, and may actually contribute to the onset of illness. In fact, feelings of despair have been suggested as one mechanism for the development of heart disease.

3. Person-Situation Interaction

Some of you may now be wondering how you react to stress. Perhaps you're aware of how your reactions to a particular situation may be very different from your best friend or spouse. You've heard the expression, "one man's meat is another man's poison." How do we account for the differences in how two people react to the same situation?

The key seems to lie in the notion of individual differences in relation to specific situations. Perhaps the most relevant example of this kind of relationship is that of the Type A (coronary prone) behavior pattern. The Type A construct was developed by two cardiologists, Drs. Ray Rosenman and Meyer Friedman in the mid-1950's. The behavior of Type A individuals is characterized by extremes of competitiveness, ambition, and aggressiveness. Type A people are often referred to as "workaholics" because of their tendency to work long hours day in and day out, while feeling guilty if they are not working. They are also likely to suffer from "hurry sickness"; they have a greatly accelerated behavioral tempo: They eat quickly, walk quickly and talk quickly. They often feel a chronic sense of time urgency—a feeling that there are just not enough hours in the day to accomplish everything that they want to do. Haste, impatience, explosiveness of speech, tenseness of facial musculature—all are often observed in Type A individuals. However, not all aspects of this syndrome need to be present for a person to be classified as possessing it. It is not a personality type per se, nor is it a standard stress response. Rather, the behavior of the Type A individual is the reaction of a person characterologically predisposed to this behavior in a particular situation that challenges him or her. The converse, Type B behavior pattern is usually defined by an absence of Type A characteristics. Type B people are often easily identified by their calm, relaxed manner and non-aggressive, non-competitive attitude.

Type A behavior is readily identified by observing the individual in action. It is displayed in speech style, motoric gestures and movements, and style of interpersonal interaction. Tom is a typical Type A. He is 43 years old and is currently the head of a large corporation. He walks briskly and always is "watching his watch" so that he won't be late for one of his frequent meetings. His speech is rapid and he often emphasizes key words in his discussions, by loudly accenting words or phrases. Some of his colleagues find him somewhat domineering; he will frequently become impatient if he feels that they are not completing their jobs fast enough, and he will even step in to do their work himself. He hates waiting on lines, and has been known to walk out of restaurants if service is too slow. His competitive attitude is easily observed: he states, "if you're not on top in this business then you shouldn't be in it." Intensity characterizes his work and his play.

The relationship between Type A behavior and heart disease has become increasingly recognized by research scientists and physicians. A number of studies have now shown an association between greater rates of coronary disease among Type A individuals. In 1960, a large scale longitudinal study was conducted in California. The project, known as the Western Collaborative Group Study, evaluated more than 3,500 men every year for ten years. Initially the men were rated as Type A or Type B and also underwent extensive medical evaluation including stress testing. The results are summarized in Fig. 21. More than 250 men who were initially healthy developed heart attacks during the course of the study.

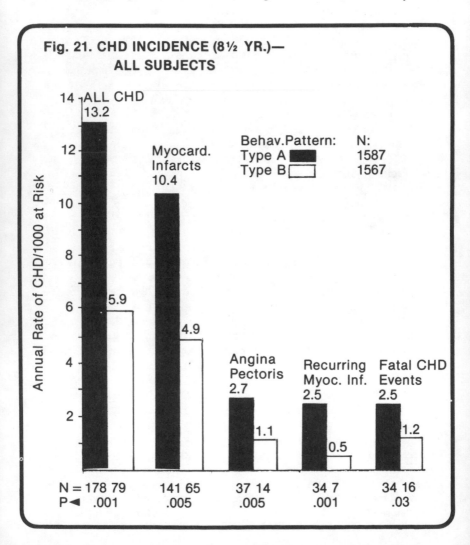

Fig. 21. CHD INCIDENCE (8½ YR.)— ALL SUBJECTS

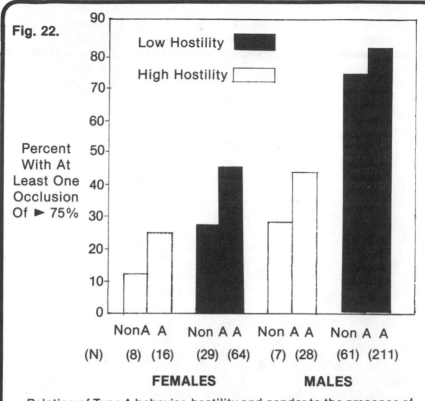

Fig. 22.

Relation of Type A behavior, hostility and gender to the presence of significant coronary artery disease (reprinted from Williams, R. B., Haney, T., Lee, K., Kong. Y., Blumenthal, J.A., and Whalen, R. E.: Type A behavior, hostility and coronary atherosclerosis. *Psychosomatic Medicine,* 1980, 42: 539-549.

Type A subjects were found to have more than twice the rate of heart attacks compared to those subjects initially judged to be Type B. Moreover, Type A individuals had twice as much angina pectoris (chest pain) and more than five times the rate of recurrent, or second, heart attacks.

Researchers at Duke University have attempted to extend these findings by relating the Type A behavior pattern to coronary artery disease. Patients who were undergoing diagnostic coronary angiography served as subjects for our research. They completed a series of psychological questionnaires immediately following the angiography procedures. We were particularly interested in the role of hostility as an independent component of the Type A behavior pattern in its relationship to coronary disease.

Subjects were considered to have significant coronary artery disease (blockages in their coronary arteries) or were judged to be disease-free by a panel of expert cardiologists. Similarly, subjects were rated as Type A or Type B, and classified as "high hostile" or "low hostile" based upon their scores on a psychological questionnaire. The results of the study showed that men had more disease than women, Type A's had more disease than Type B's, and "high hostile" subjects had more disease that did "low hostile" subjects. The composite results of the study are summarized in Fig. 22. As you can see, the low hostile, Type B women were least likely to have significant coronary artery disease, while the hostile Type A men were most likely to have significant disease. This study demonstrates the importance of individual characteristics (i.e., Type A behavior and hostility) in relation to heart disease. Moreover, specific situations such as those involving frustration or competition seem to be important in eliciting Type A behavior and hostility. It is this interaction between an individual's personal characteristics and certain stress-producing situations that may be responsible for the higher rates of heart disease found among Type A individuals.

Guidelines for successful coping

We conclude that the effects that a particular situation may have on a person depends on how that person copes with the situation as much as the situation itself. Ineffective coping can take a variety of forms. For example, some people behave in ways that directly impair their health: they overeat, overdrink, oversmoke, and overwork. They may engage in other, less direct, maladaptive behaviors such as worrying, not sleeping, maintaining a poor diet, or not exercising. Other indirect effects include the maintenance of chronic states of arousal that Cannon and later Selye described in their work.

Stress is a complex problem for which there is no easy solution. Certainly engaging in regular exercise, eating a nutritious diet, maintaining proper personal hygiene, getting adequate sleep, developing satisfying relationships, and participating in recreational activities are all important and necessary. There are also specific techniques that you can learn to handle stress successfully.

Behavioral training designed to enhance adaptive coping strategies often emphasizes a combination of cognitive (e.g., planning a course of action, reducing irrelevant thoughts, waiting patiently, etc.) and physiological (e.g., muscular relaxation) techniques.

Step 1: Appropriate Help-seeking and Information Gathering

Learning information about a stressful situation is an important technique for coping with stress effectively. For example, learning how to prepare for a public speech is helpful in giving talks before large audiences. Another example is that of the man who spent two months worrying about chest pain he was experiencing during exercise. Fearful that he may have a heart condition, he spent many hours at home and at work worrying about his condition. A simple visit to his physician could have provided him with the information necessary for him to plan an appropriate course of action.

Step 2: Learning Constructive Self-statements
Cognitions, or thoughts about ourselves frequently take the form of self-statements. What we say to ourselves makes a difference in how we behave! For example, an individual who responds to his boss's criticism by telling himself that it is a catastrophe or that he is worthless or incompetent will have a very different physical and emotional reaction than the individual who tells himself "So I'm having an off day. I'll learn from my mistake and do better next time." It is important to learn to identify your own "self-statements." Increasing your awareness about what you say to yourself is a first step. As you become more aware, you can then try to stop negative statements and substitute positive statements. You'll be surprised what a difference this small change can make!

Step 3: Learning to Recognize Stress
Keep a daily diary in which you note your experience of stress during the week. You will notice feelings of tension, nervousness, frustration and impatience. Also pay careful attention to situations that contribute to these feelings. The goal of successful "stress management" is to reduce or eliminate unpleasant feelings that you experience in these situations and to substitute more pleasant and adaptive responses. One way you may learn to become more aware of your tension level is to regularly rate your tension levels on a scale of 1 to 10 throughout the day. Let 1 represent complete relaxation, and 10 represent the most tension you ever experienced. What is your level of tension right at this moment? If you pause throughout the day to rate your tension level you will be surprised as to how much variation in tension levels you experience.

Step 4: Learning to Relax
The history of relaxation training dates back more than 4,000 years to ancient China. Our more contemporary relaxation procedures are generally credited to the work of Edmund Jacobson. Jacobson developed his technique called progressive muscle relaxation training in 1934 at Harvard University. His early work on stress showed that emotional tension creates shortening of muscle fibers which can be counteracted by teaching people to do the exact opposite: relax their muscles. His procedure involves the systematic tensing and releasing of various muscle groups throughout the body and thereby learning to discriminate and control muscular tension.
The ability to relax deeply and quickly is an extremely useful cop-

ing response in dealing with stress. The following procedure should allow you to learn this important self-control behavior within two weeks. Once mastered, the relaxation response can be used to cope with stress or tension as soon as you feel it beginning to occur.

It is recommended that these relaxation exercises be practiced at least twice a day until they are mastered. The exercises will initially require about thirty minutes of practice, but as you master the technique, the time required will become progressively shorter. ·

1. Get as comfortable as possible. Tight clothing should be loosened and your legs should not be crossed. Take a deep breath, let it out slowly, and become as relaxed as possible.

2. Raise your arms and extend them out in front of you. Now make a fist with both hands as hard as you can. Notice the uncomfortable tension in your hands and fingers. Hold the tension for five seconds, then let the tension out half way and hold for an additional five seconds. Notice the decrease in tension but also concentrate on the tension that is still present. Then let your hands relax completely. Notice how the tension and discomfort drain from your hands and are replaced by sensations of comfort and relaxation. Focus on the contrast between the tension you created and the contrasting state of relaxation you now feel. Concentrate on relaxing your hands completely for 15 seconds.

3. Tense your biceps hard for five seconds by bending your arms at the elbow. Focus on the feeling of tension. Then let the tension out half way for an additional five seconds. Again, focus on the tension that is still present. Now relax your upper arms completely for 15 seconds and focus carefully on the developing sense of relaxation.

4. Bend your hands at the wrist, extending your fingers upward as far as possible. Hold the tension for five seconds, then let the tension out half way for an additional five seconds. Now relax the muscles completely and concentrate on the relaxation until they are completely loose and relaxed.

5. Now tense your neck muscles by bringing your head forward until your chin digs into your chest. Hold for five seconds, release the tension half way for another five seconds, and then relax your neck completely. Allow your head to hang comfortably while you focus on the relaxation developing in your neck muscles.

6. Tense your upper shoulders by "shrugging" your shoulders —try to touch your shoulders to your ears. Let the tension out half way and hold for five seconds, and then relax completely. Let your shoulders drop down and get completely relaxed.

7. Push your shoulders back as far as possible so as to tense your back muscles. Let the tension out half way after five seconds, and then relax your back and shoulder muscles completely. Focus on the spreading relaxation until they are completely relaxed.

8. Now move to the muscles of your face. First, wrinkle your

solution to complex problems of everyday life. However, it does represent a simple technique which can have significant value when used in an appropriate manner. This is well illustrated by the case of a successful business executive who came to the author because of "stress and tension" which had likely contributed to his heart condition. Although he was only in his early forties, he had significant coronary artery disease and recently underwent open heart surgery. He described himself as a typical Type A personality: uptight, impatient, and restless. He was taking tranquilizers several times a day and often used alcohol to calm himself down.

While relaxation training should not be construed as a cure for heart disease, the patient agreed to participate in a series of six sessions of relaxation training in order to discontinue his reliance on drugs and alcohol for tension relief. After only a month of training and regular practice he was able to consistently and reliably achieve a deep state of muscular relaxation. He was able to recognize even minor increases in tension and could frequently identify the source of his stress. He also was able to slow down his behavioral tempo; he walked more slowly, ate more slowly, and did not become nearly as frustrated or impatient as he had previously. Interestingly, an unexpected side effect of his treatment was increased marital satisfaction. His wife and children reported that he became much easier to live with. While relaxation may not have been directly responsible for this change, it most likely facilitated his new attitude.

Friedrich Nietzsche once remarked, "what doesn't destroy me makes me strong." Learning to cope effectively with stress can make you strong. As you learn to cope better with difficult situations you will gain in self-confidence and deal more effectively with future stresses. It is said that the word for stress in Chinese combines symbols for the words danger and opportunity. Let stress be and opportunity for you—the key is successful coping!

7

Overweight
Its Origin and Treatment

Siegfried Heyden, M.D.
Barbara Stucky

The most common excuse doctors hear from overweight patients is that of inheritance: "I can't help it. Overweight runs in my family." Medical research in the last decade has disproved this "inheritance" theory. If obesity seems to "run in families", the reason is not genetic but culinary. The patient has inherited the unwise cooking, including recipes, and eating habits of the previous generation. The second most common excuse is the "heavy bones" theory, and it should be laid to rest beside the first excuse. Studies have shown that even truly obese people have completely normal bone structure. It is easy to determine a patient's original bone structure by the circumference of his wrists and ankles. The fat arm or leg still allows an estimation of the usually small or medium framed wrist and ankle. Furthermore, the many extra pounds of an obese person cannot be explained by the few extra ounces of calcium contained in bigger bones nor by the greater muscle mass of a large-boned person. Another common "explanation" is: "There's something wrong with my glands." Glandular imbalance, and endocrine disorder like hypofunction of the thyroid as a cause of overweight is found in, at most, one-half of one percent (0.05%) of all overweight people. It is true that female hormones do influence the accumulation of fluid but never to the extent many women believe. A considerable number of women do gain weight after the menopause when ovarian hormone production is reduced to a minimum. But it should be kept in mind that this is a time when most women are less physically active than before, while maintaining, or even increasing, their calorie intake.

The cause of overweight is overeating the wrong foods, the intake of excess calories and the failure to expand a sufficient amount of calories through physical activity. While we usually underestimate the caloric value of food, most of us overestimate the calories burned in any type of activity on the job or in leisure time.

The first principle of weight reduction is: reduce the amount of table salt (i.e., sodium chloride) in the diet. Take for example the case of the 603-lb. man. He was admitted to the clinic unconscious and in a life threatening condition, which is called the Pickwick syndrome. It is caused by an elevation of the diaphragm. This "pushing" of the diaphragm up by the excess fat in the abdomen causes severe limitation of pulmonary expansion. This, in turn, creates a serious problem in the exchange between oxygen—which the body needs—and carbon dioxide—which the body is trying to get rid of. Since carbon dioxide accumulates in the brain, the patient is usually sleepy, semiconscious or may even die in a coma. After ten days on a salt-free liquid diet (water, coffee, tea and other non-caloric fluids), he had lost a total of 75 pounds (34 kilos). This weight loss represented a loss of 75 pounds of water. The explanation of this weight loss is simple: with the liquid intake he received no water-retaining salt or sodium chloride. On a diet of ample, calorie-free fluids his body was able to flush out the excess salt from his fat cells.

Each fat cell may increase eight times its original size. About 50% of its content is made up from fat, the other half from salt and water. These cells, once rid of excess salt, naturally lose water and become reduced in size. By the third day of hospitalization this patient practically never left the bathroom; and this man no longer experienced fatigue and sleepiness. Granted, this individual's case was extreme, but he illustrates the first rule of weight reduction; strict limitation of sodium chloride. This rule applies equally to people who are only moderately overweight; every overweight person automatically retains salt which in turn binds the water inside each fat cell. With every 100 or 1000 extra, unnecessary calories consumed, excess salt is consumed as well and is stored in the body. Overweight persons should restrict their sodium salt intake to the limited amount already found in *unprocessed* and uncanned meat, fish and fowl, fresh vegetables, and skim milk products.

One special point must be made. It concerns the restriction of sodium for women. Women dieters should be especially careful about reintroducing limited amounts of salt into their diets if they notice symptoms of puffiness, swelling, edema, headaches. This generally occurs 3 to 4 days before a period, with a tendency to store salt and thus retention of water, which may lead to swelling of fingers and feet and tenderness or outright painful sensations in the breasts. The use of salt and salty foods should be avoided at this time. Patients with high blood pressure should, of course, maintain a low-salt diet at all times.

The second principle of weight reduction is: reduce certain carbohydrates. The main sources of carbohydrates are vegetables, fruits, starches, and bread, but carbohydrates are also present in milk products. Vegetables, fruits and skim milk products are no problem, however, initially, bread, and all other starches or flour-based products and whole milk products should be eliminated from the menu of any weight-loss diet. Why? Every livestock farmer knows that a diet of carbohydrate-rich feed results in increased fat deposits in his animals because the grain, bread, potatoes and other carbohydrate left-overs from the farmer's table are converted into fat within 24 hours. This applies as well to sedentary people who consume too many carbohydrates.

Carbohydrates not only affect body fat, but also blood sugar. Not all carbohydrates are equally "dangerous." The five symbols in Fig. 23. graphically illustrate how sugar and sugar containing

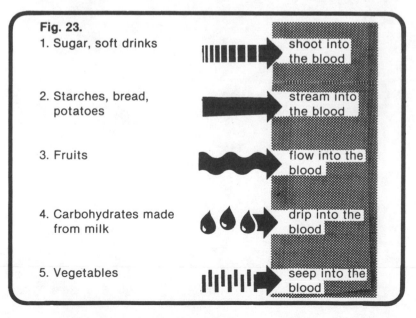

Fig. 23.
1. Sugar, soft drinks — shoot into the blood
2. Starches, bread, potatoes — stream into the blood
3. Fruits — flow into the blood
4. Carbohydrates made from milk — drip into the blood
5. Vegetables — seep into the blood

products practically shoot into the blood stream, how carbohydrates from bread, starches and potatoes stream directly into the bloodstream; in sharp contrast, carbohydrates from vegetables (at the bottom) slowly seep into the blood and cause a minimal rise, if any, in blood sugar levels. Carbohydrates from fruits flow into the blood circulation and those from milk products enter the blood stream drop by drop. Milk products from skim milk are very useful in the diets of overweight persons.

To show why any reducing diet must restrict the consumption of all starches, let's see what happens to the blood sugar level of an overweight person when he eats a small breakfast of two slices of bread and jam, and coffee with sugar. In a *normal weight person,* at the moment the sugar, jam and bread touch the tongue, an order goes to the pancreas to produce insulin to slow down the ascending blood sugar level. The blood sugar levels rise to approximately 150 mg% (lower of the two curves), and within the next two hours insulin reduces the blood sugar level to the amount measured *at the fasting state.* To emphasize, this is the normal blood sugar cycle of someone of normal weight whose system can easily handle a meal rich in carbohydrates.

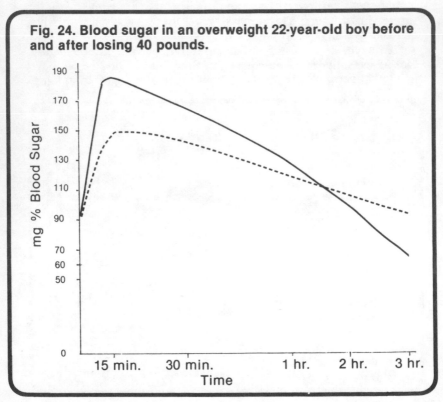

Fig. 24. Blood sugar in an overweight 22-year-old boy before and after losing 40 pounds.

In contrast, what happens to the blood sugar curve in an overweight body? By following the upper curve, you can trace the rise of the blood sugar level. The fasting level of this overweight person is 97 mg%—the upper limit of the norm. But within 15 minutes after the carbohydrate-rich meal of bread, jam and sugar, the blood level has reached 185 mg%. This does not mean that the overweight person is a diabetic, but it is characteristic of overweight people that their bodies have developed a resistance to insulin. For lack of a better term, the medical profession talks about an "insulin block" which quite accurately describes the fact that insulin is there—but it does not come out when it is needed. What occurs in this case is that *after* the blood sugar level has markedly risen—in this case to over 180 mg%—there is a belated but massive mobilization of insulin. This phenomenon is called hyper (too much)-insulinemia (insulin in the blood), which rapidly reduces the blood sugar level within the next three hours to such a low (65 mg%) that the overweight person becomes *hypoglycemic,* that is suffering from a sub-normal blood sugar level. We saw that on an empty stomach the overweight person had a blood sugar level of 97 mg%. Three hours after a carbohydrate-rich breakfast, his blood sugar has plummeted from 185 mg%, 120 units down to 65 mg%. During this "dive", the body of an overweight person experiences a number of typical, unpleasant sensations: cluster headaches which do not respond to aspirin, fatigue, uneasiness, cold sweats, trembling and hunger. This condition is often described by fat people as "something's gone wrong with my body." As the blood sugar level plunges, they feel a compulsion to eat something, preferably rich in carbohydrates, in order to quickly raise the blood sugar again. After a piece of bread, candy, chocolate, coke or plain sugar, the overweight person experiences a feeling of satisfaction—at first because the blood sugar is way up again. But three to four hours later he feels as though he were starving. And in fact, as long as he eats food rich in carbohydrates, he is in a vicious circle and will be intensely hungry every three to four hours.

These wild swings in his blood sugar curve from too high to too low can only be avoided if the overweight person abstains from certain carbohydrates. When this same overweight person loses 40 pounds (almost 20 kilos), his blood sugar level when fasting will be at 93 mg%, and after the same breakfast of carbohydrates will reach a peak of 150 mg%—a normal level. After three hours his original blood sugar level of 93 mg% will be reached, because insulin was mobilized at the right time, that is, immediately following the carbohydrate intake; thus insulin prevented the blood sugar from rising any higher. Only after an overweight person loses roughly 40 pounds (approximately 20 kilos), and/or attains his normal weight, then and only then can he start adding carbohydrates from bread and starches to his diet. It is really irrelevant whether an overweight person consumes 20 or 30 or 50 calories in sugar or foods containing sugar. Whether 20 or 50 calories, these sugar calories all cause the blood sugar of an overweight person to shoot up high. Consequently, sugar, whether in the form of canned fruits and juices, cookies, cakes or refined sugar as a sweetening, should be cut from the dieter's menus until the patient's normal weight has been reached. In the first few months of a weight reduction program, this same strictness should also apply to bread and *all* starches (farinaceous products).

This ban on bread evokes heart-wrenching pleas: "If I have to give up my sweet roll and biscuit for breakfast, couldn't I have just a piece of bread? I can't even have that? Then at least a piece of Rye-Krisp!" At the risk of assuming the role of a pitiless warder, the doctor must convince the patient of the temporary necessity of placing on the diet blacklist all carbohydrates from bread and flour-based products. In a necessarily calorie-reduced diet for the purpose of weight reduction, there is no place for empty calories like starches, cokes, etc.

But not only a knife and fork are self-destructive tools in the hands of an overweight person; contents of glasses are a danger to him too. Alcohol, whether beer or wine, brandy or whiskey, contains many empty calories and has no place in a reducing diet, no matter how miniscule the quantity. Alcohol calories should be spurned until the dieter's weight has normalized. Each gram of regular carbohydrates contains 4 calories, however, each gram of alcohol contains 7 calories! The dieter should concentrate on the calories contained in protein and carbohydrates from vegetables and fruit.

Having enumerated a number of eat-nots, we would like to offer some positive diet suggestions. Because vegetable carbohydrates seep slowly into the bloodstream, we would like to recommend a 150 calorie soup as a satisfying meal. A vegetable-meat soup's calorie content is dispersed as follows: 1 oz. lean beef or 1½ oz. of chicken (without skin)—60 calories; ½ cup each of cooked carrots, asparagus, red cabbage, cauliflowers and green peppers—15 to 20 calories per ½ cup for each vegetable. This soup takes relatively little time to prepare, and can be varied with a number of different vegetables as long as the calorie limits are maintained. The combination of ingredients is important, because the amount of meat is just enough to make the soup savoury. With the addition of salt-free spices—ground pepper, curry or diet aroma—the soup dinner can be made even more tasty.

A suggestion for a summer meal is a mixed salad. For once we can be lavish. Spinach leaves, fresh mushrooms, finely sliced, and cucumber add up to less than 100 calories; 25 cucumber slices have only 20 calories. With the aid of a calorie table the dieter can use his imagination to invent other salad combinations. One small helping of lettuce translates into 5 calories. The addition of 1 tablespoon of oil increases the calorie total by 95, but one needn't use a whole tablespoon. A mixed salad is a dieter's delight: Boston lettuce, 1 green pepper, 2 medium tomatoes, 4 radishes, chopped onion if desired, vinegar, dill and diet mustard (free of sodium). Even though it uses only one teaspoon of oil (45 calories) it is deliciously satisfying, contains only 150 calories and the chewing time is exactly 20 minutes. A further plus of salads like this is that they contain vitamins and trace elements which are an important part of any diet. The replacement of some of the above ingredients with cottage cheese or water-packed tuna fish makes salads even better. The only limit to the salad maker's imagination is a calorie counter and, of course, the salad dressing.

Fresh fruits are as much of a dieter's mainstay as fresh vegetables, although attention should be paid to their caloric content as they do vary, and fruit calories *do* count. Instead of a fattening dessert, a 150 calorie fruit salad can be substituted:

½ large peach
½ large orange
⅓ banana
½ cup fresh strawberries

Fruit salads can be varied and made even more piquant by adding 3 oz. of red currants (35 cals.) or 3 oz. of unsugared raspberries (40 cals.)

The third principle of weight reduction is: eat protein-rich foods. Fish, lean beef and veal are highly recommended, as are chicken and turkey—with one important qualification. The skin of fowl is rich in fat and cholesterol; it must always be removed. Skim milk products (cottage cheese, yogurt, low fat cheese) are highly recommended because they contain all the protein, vitamins A and D, and calcium as in whole milk products but the fat has been removed! Egg whites are particularly good on a weight reduction diet because the amino acid-protein content simulates mother's milk, perfect for the rebuilding of cells. One egg white = 15 calories. Unlike carbohydrate-rich meals, protein-rich food has virtually no influence on blood sugar levels. Tests were done on the blood sugar of ten men, each of whom had eaten a protein-rich meal. Results demonstrated that food rich in protein has practically no influence on blood sugar levels. Protein meals produce insulin in minute amounts. Results thus established that blood sugar levels were neither raised nor lowered. Protein provides the ideal food of overweight people: for breakfast, egg whites and a protein-rich cereal with skim milk, for lunch fish, and for dinner skinless chicken or turkey.

As these menu suggestions have shown, it is possible to lose weight without an attending loss in taste or nourishment. A breakfast of two egg *whites* lightly fried with a half teaspoon of margarine totals only 55 calories (2 X 15 cals. for egg whites plus 25 cals. for the margarine) and is filling, but causes no concomitant rise in blood sugar. (Egg yolks contain too much fat and cholesterol to be used in this diet system: One yolk contains 300 mg. of cholesterol and, in addition 65 cals.) Another breakfast suggestion is a small bowl of unsugared cereal flakes, preferably of the bran type, with a half cup of skim milk which adds up to only 150 calories. A further advantage of a breakfast like this is the fact that one will not be "starving" three hours later, as one would be after a calorie-loaded meal of carbohydrates such as rolls, bread, toast or biscuits, not to mention "Danish", muffins, cookies or cakes etc.

A further "no" is fats, and in particular, "hidden" fats. The peanut provides a vivid example of the calories in fats. A small package of peanuts contains not only a large quantity of salt, but also an almost unbelievable number of calories—over 400. A slice of chocolate cake has about 500 calories, most of which come, not from the sugar and flour alone, but from the butter and eggs used. Other examples of foods to avoid for their hidden salt, fats and their attendant calories—real land mines in the dieter's 'garden'—are pizza, fried chicken, potato chips, cheese-and other burgers, hot dogs, etc.

To emphasize, the dieter must say "yes" to fresh vegetables, salads and fruits, to herbs, spices, and the proteins from egg whites, from skim milk and its products, from fowl and lean meats. He must learn to say "no" to carbohydrates other than fruits and vegetables and to table and "hidden" salts.

No one realistically expects a person with a long history of over-eating to turn overnight into an iron-willed ascetic. **We can therefore add a fourth principle of weight reduction which can help compensate for the occasional relapse into bad eating habits: have a weekly zero calorie day.** On this date of fasting only abundant amounts of no-cal liquids should be consumed. As an example of how this works, take the case of a physically inactive male of average weight, who must carefully watch his intake in order not to gain weight. His normal caloric intake is about 2,000. But on Friday evening he snacks on peanuts and beer: 1,000 extra calories. Saturday evening he is invited to dinner, during the course of which he "overloads" an approximate 1,000 more excess calories. In order to reduce his mild over-weight of 2 to 4 pounds (1 to 2 kilos), he would be advised to fast on Sunday by drinking tea, coffee, water or no-cal drinks. By the following day he will be down to his normal weight level. One "no-cal" day a week allows the dieter an occasional splurge and helps overcome the psychological barrier of feeling "deprived." Interestingly, almost all world religions know the value of and are using fasting (Yom Kippur) or semi-fasting (Rhamadan) or reduced caloric intake (some Christian sects 40 days prior to Easter), but this is not widely practiced in our part of the world.

We summarize the suggestions that have been made for losing weight: restriction of salt and replacement by herbs and spices; reduction of carbohydrates to 60 grams per day, 60 grams of protein-rich food daily and 25 grams of fat per day (paying attention to "hidden" fats). These amounts reckoned in calories mean *240 calories of carbohydrates, 240 calories of proteins* and *225 of fats.* This total of 700 calories is just enough for an inactive obese person to lose some weight every day. With the adoption of one "No-Cal" day a week, the obese patient will lose about 2 lbs. (1 kilo) a week. The 700 calories may be distributed as follows: Breakfast—150 calories; Lunch—400 calories; Dinner—150 calories (or Lunch—150 calories; Dinner—400 calories); if breakfast is not taken, it may be consumed as a late night snack not exceeding 150 calories.

As a reinforcement to the patient's will power (and memory), a diet diary should be kept in which everything which is eaten or drunk should be entered. At the top of each day's page the patient should enter his weight before breakfast. The morning "weigh-in" should become as fixed and matter-of-fact a habit as brushing one's teeth. In case of constipation, we advise the use of glycerine suppositories rather than oral laxatives.

One final point concerns working fat off in exercise. The lack of physical exercise is one of the risk factors of our affluent society. Physical activity is excellent for improving one's circulation and muscle tone and is certainly recommended for everyone, except patients with abnormal treadmill EKG's who would need to be reconditioned under the supervision of a physician. The number of calories used in varying kinds of physical activity is generally less than we *think.* For example, it takes 45 minutes of walking to "work off" the calories contained in only 2 Brazil nuts or 1½ hours of constant dancing to "get rid" of 500 calories from a rich cake with whipped cream. And after a long walk, how easy it is to nullify the calorie loss by stilling one's thirst with juices or sweetened drinks rich in calories. The role of physical exercise in a weight reduction program should not be overestimated.

8

Exercise Testing

R. Sanders Williams, M.D.

There has been a definite trend in recent years towards greater skepticism among the consumers of medical care regarding tests and procedures prescribed for them by their physicians, making the individual doctor's discretion over the expenditure of health care dollars considerably less sacrosanct. This trend has basically been a healthy one, reflecting an increased interest and sophistication among the general public regarding health-related issues, and producing greater scrutiny among physicians regarding the true value and cost-effectiveness of many tests and procedures which are part of common medical practice in the United States today. The exercise stress test is one such procedure which has attracted special attention, particularly concerning its role as a screening procedure for coronary artery disease in adults who are free of symptoms. The select Committee on Exercise of the American Heart Association recommends exercise stress testing for adults over the age of thirty-five who wish to begin an exercise program; however, widely circulated periodicals such as Runners' World have published editorials entitled "Bypass the Stress Test", and an informal pool of physician joggers revealed only a minority who had undergone stress testing themselves.

Why the confusion and controversy? To begin, let's analyze how stress testing is performed. The most common procedure practiced today involves the subject walking on a treadmill while an electrocardiogram is monitored and recorded. In general, the speed and grade of the treadmill are increased as the test proceeds, requiring increasingly greater effort from the subject, until fatigue, symptoms, or abnormal changes in blood pressure, pulse rate, or the electrocardiogram occur. Exercise produced by stepping up and down stairs, by riding a stationary bicycle, or by handgrip are also employed occasionally for stress testing, but less commonly than the treadmill. Persons who have narrowing of one or more of the arteries of the heart, as the work demands upon the heart increase, will often develop areas of the heart muscle which become short of oxygen, and this lack of oxygen, or "ischemia", is associated with changes in the electrocardiogram. However, it is clear that exercise electrocardiography, even in its most sophisticated modern forms, cannot diagnose the presence or absence of coronary artery disease in the same manner that a blood count can diagnose anemia, or that a throat culture can diagnose a strep throat. For reasons that remain unclear to cardiologists, persons with completely normal hearts may occasionally develop abnormalities in their electrocardiogram during exercise which are indistinguishable from the changes seen in persons with severe obstructions of one or more arteries of the heart. Likewise, persons with extensive heart disease may occasionally have a completely normal electrocardiogram at rest, and during exercise stress. These "false postive", and "false negative" tests can lead to erroneous diagnoses, especially if the imperfections of the test are ignored, or if the treadmill test is not interpreted in light of the total clinical picture.

Do these problems mean that the exercise stress test is without value entirely? Absolutely not; despite its limitations, important information can be derived from exercise stress testing in several stiuations. For example, in patients who are already known to have coronary artery disease, stress testing is essential in determining the functional significance of blockages in the coronary arteries, and in assessing the effects of treatment, whether by medications, rehabilitative exercise programs, or by surgery. Furthermore, there is evidence that exercise stress testing may yield important information regarding a person's risk for developing heart attack within the one-year period following the test independently of whether the exercise electrocardiogram was abnormal or normal. In a recent study persons who achieved high work levels during treadmill testing had an almost negligible chance of death from heart attack within one year, even if they had abnormal coronary arteries, whereas persons who had to stop at very low treadmill work levels had a very poor prognosis, and often had extensive coronary blockages, even if the exercise electrocardiogram showed no abnormalities.

We continue to recommend exercise stress testing to persons over thirty-five years of age who plan a dramatic change in their exercise habits, even in the absence of symptoms, despite the recognized shortcomings of the test. Any abnormalities detected during stress testing, whether they involve abnormal changes in the electrocardiogram, abnormal blood pressure or heart rate responses, or the inability to exercise past low work levels are interpreted in light of the other clinical findings such as age, sex, family history, or associated medical problems. At the current time other forms of exercise testing which involve scanning the heart following the injection of radioactive tracers are being investigated, and these techniques promise to be helpful in extending our ability to diagnose coronary heart disease by techniques less dangerous and expensive than cardiac catheterization. These newer forms of exercise stress testing have their own limitations however, and for the time being, the injection of dye into the arteries of the heart at the time of cardiac catheterization remains the definitive diagnostic procedure.

In summary, exercise stress testing can provide important information regarding a person's overall level of physical fitness, and can be an aid in the detection of coronary artery disease. In persons with known heart disease, stress testing is extremely helpful in assessing the functional severity of the disease, and in measuring the responses to therapy. As a screening procedure for asymptomatic persons who plan to begin an exercise program, stress testing can help identify persons at high risk for the development of serious medical problems during exercise. However, a "normal" exercise electrocardiogram is no guarantee that the heart is normal, and persons with entirely normal hearts can sometimes develop "abnormal" changes in their electrocardiograms during exercise. The precise role for exercise stress testing in the diagnosis of coronary heart disease, and the cost-effectiveness of the test in identifying high-risk subjects remains a topic of extensive medical research.

9

Stop Smoking Clinics

Robert H. Shipley, Ph.D
Carole S. Orleans, Ph.D

To locate stop-smoking clinics in your area call your physician, the local chapter of the American Cancer Society, the American Heart Association, the American Lung Association, or the Psychology and Psychiatry Departments of local colleges, medical schools or hospitals. Beware of one-time clinics offered by local service organizations which consist only of a series of lectures. Only groups which repeatedly offer quit clinics gain the expertise to be effective. Also be skeptical of programs that claim outstanding success rates. Many programs can claim very high success at helping people stop smoking for a day or so, but few programs achieve long-term success (six months to a year) with over half of their participants. If you find a program claiming long-term success rates of 70% or more, chances are the person doing the counting is seeing double (or triple). Some national programs which might be available in your area are discussed below, including commercial programs which exist to make a profit and non-commercial programs run by service organizations.

In addition to the clinics listed, you should consider local clinics run by the medical or psychological professions. These clinics vary widely in their techniques, costs, and effectiveness. Many are very good. For example, the California Kaiser Foundation offers clinics at a nominal fee ($15-$45 for members, $30-$85 for nonmembers). Similar clinics are offered by the Palo Alto Health Education Center and by the Toronto City Health Department. Long-term success rates for these clinics have been good (30-50% at one year).

Noncommercial Clinics

Clinics run by voluntary health organizations use health education and group support and offer practical suggestions on how to quit. Not much research has been done on the effectiveness of these clinics. However, about six out of ten people quit smoking, with about two out of ten people still not smoking one year later. These figures count as failures people who drop out of the clinics before completing the program. If you complete an entire clinic, your chances for success will be higher. Soliciting the aid of your physician, in addition to attending a quit clinic, can also boost your chance for long-term success.

The Seventh Day Adventist Five-Day Plan uses five consecutive two-hour group sessions. In the sessions, films are shown to demonstrate the health effects of cigarettes, there are lectures and demonstrations, and a buddy support system is set up. Participants are taught ways to deal with withdrawal effects by doing things such as increasing water intake, omitting coffee, and using deep breathing for tension control. Group leaders include professionals such as physicians, nurses, psychologists and pastors who have had brief training in the Five-Day plan.

The American Cancer Society sponsors quit-smoking clinics through its local chapters. Three treatment phases occur in twice-weekly one-and-a-half hour sessions over a four-week interval: assessment of the smoking habit; practicing quitting under controlled conditions; and maintaining abstinence. Group leaders instruct members in how to cope with withdrawal symptoms, avoid activities that lead to smoking, and reward nonsmoking. A buddy support system is also used. Group leaders are generally nonprofessionals who have been briefly trained. Many groups also have local specialists give talks on selected topics.

Commercial Clinics

The old saying "you get what you pay for" has some significance when it is noted that commercial clinics report one-year success rates of about 35-55%; twice as effective as non-profit programs. Perhaps the high fees they charge assure that only those who truly want to stop smoking enroll. Some commercial organizations, motivated by the profit motive, do provide psychologically-sound programs that are more intensive and lengthier than those offered by noncommercial clinics.

SmokEnders, for instance, uses a gradual reduction technique which emphasizes rewards for accomplishments. They wisely avoid fear-arousing measures. Nine weekly group sessions are held, with a participant asked to stop smoking at the fifth week of treatment. They then attend additional meetings if they wish. The present charge for SmokEnders is about $300.00. Group leaders are ex-smokers who have been trained by SmokEnders.

Smoke Watchers assigns cut-down goals at weekly group meetings. Participants follow a text discussing the various aspects of smoking behavior. The number of treatment sessions varies at different locations. Current charges vary from $10-$25 for the initial membership fee and $5.00-$7.50 per meeting.

Schick Centers for the Control of Smoking attempt to condition an aversion to smoking by having participants over-smoke, puff rapidly on a cigarette, and receive mild electric shocks paired with smoking behaviors. Treatments occur on five consecutive days, followed by eight weeks of education on nutrition, weight control, relaxation, aerobics, behavior modification, and goal achievement. Meetings are attended twice a week in the first two weeks, and once a week thereafter. Participants may attend any of the educational sessions they wish. People who resume smoking during the first year after a clinic may return to treatment without additional charge. The fee for the clinic is about $500; a refund is available to participants who have not stopped smoking by the fifth day of treatment. However, as in most treatments, the problem is not stopping but staying off cigarettes over a period of time. Consequently, only 6% of clients request a refund. Leaders are non-professional graduates of the treatment program who have been given two weeks of training. In our opinion, the aversive treatment components may present a health risk to people with heart or lung disorders, and you should check with your physician if you have reason to question your physical fitness for this treatment.